THE UNSUNG HERO

OF PAKISTAN

SUSAN HILL

First Published (Printed) in August 2019

First Published (e-book) in August 2018

ISBN: 978-1-54396-831-6

ASIN: B07GZT3TGY (e-book)

Table of Contents

The Unsung Hero of Pakistan

There are so many people in Pakistan who are a source of inspiration and motivation for the rest of their fellow citizens. Most of these people are those who signify their countries on both global and national level and bring splendor and dignity to their respective countries. They are distinguished with laurels and awards. Though most of them don't get recognition and honor as much as they deserved. These are our unsung heroes.

This book was motivated by the desire we and others have had to achieve our dreams and success in our lives. Tariq's life begin when he was born in Bharatpur, India. This book is the result of struggles and achievement Tariq made throughout his life. You may think you have lived an unremarkable life, but succeeding generations will be interested in hearing it. What you consider normal and mundane will be interesting and slightly unusual to them. This book is the first heartfelt eyewitness account of Tariq's life before India Pakistan partition and after. He wrote in his autobiography about the partition bloodshed and what he has achieved as a Badminton Champion. He lived it, so to him, it was normal and mundane, but to his children, it is a tale from history. Partition, as Tariq observes, divided the Subcontinent into India and Pakistan along with separating it from its colonial past. Some historians may go even further and look at Partition inherently as the partition of Indian Muslims, who now remain divided into three nation-states and which ironically lack the sort of channels that might encourage crucial and substantial cross-boundary contacts.

The migration has left so many transformative imprints on the life of Tariq. In his journey of becoming a Badminton Champion, he got the chance to fulfill his childhood dream. When he started playing for Pakistan that is when he thought someday he would be on the top of the world. Learning from your mistakes and coming back much stronger is the important thing that is what he felt and that's how he learnt and came up in his life.

We hope Tariq's journey and passion would encourage you to take actions in fulfilling your dreams too!

Introduction

Unlike their portrayal in popular culture, heroes have no fixed templates. They might not always pop out at you with their rising capes, larger-than-life personalities, and overnight revolutions. Instead, you might have to look around carefully to find those undiscovered visionaries. Tariq is one of the silent crusaders of Pakistan spent his life serving his country. Tariq from a very early age, representing his school and college at the start then slowly rising through the ranks from district player to state and finally reached a national level. He was unknown to the World then, not until he made the breakthrough in national games through sheer hard work and determination and of course talent plays a part as well. And most importantly, he took the chance when there was an opening and this separates the players who made it and those who don't.

For many of us, life is a struggle. Unless you are lucky, you will have periods in your life where things will not go your way. But for Tariq life is a series of beautiful struggles which give rise to joy. Without growth, life would be dull and dreary. We strive and struggle so that we may overcome – for it is in overcoming that we prevail and realize our magnificence. Tariq's life is filled with moments of bliss when he was least expecting it. The timely break that comes just in time, having devoted much of his life pursuing his passion. His struggles paled into insignificance when he fell in love with sports and committed to serving others. This book illustrates the dichotomy of Tariq's life. Without the fight, life serves no role towards our individual development.

Muhammad Tariq Khan

Early Life – A Roller Coaster of Emotions and Struggles

Born on August 14, 1942, in Bharatpur India along the floating islands and verdant green expanse, Muhammad Tariq Khan soon became one of the best "**Badminton Champion"** and fell in love with the sport at an early age. Traveling down the memory lane, Tariq remembered most vividly from his younger days in Bharatpur. He remembered the beautiful city which is located in the district of Rajasthan, situated on an immense alluvial plain with isolated hilly areas in the north and south about 35 miles (55 km) west of Agra. The city was famous for the temples, diverse avian population, and the festive zest. The weather in Bharatpur was extremely hot in summers and very cold in winters. The temperature in summers even reaches $50°$ C. And the temperature hits $0°C$ sometimes in winter. It's too sticky during the summers and rainy season and only a few months were dry," says Tariq.

The immigration that complemented India's independence and partition in 1947 was the major movement of people in human history, but nearly no one anticipated it to happen. After this partition Hindus and Muslims had begun to turn on each other during the chaos. More than millions of people were killed and most of them were displaced during partition between India and Pakistan. Both the countries were separated and the massacres begin soon after British announced the partition. Their lives, yesterdays, faiths, dreams, identities, interpersonal relations – everything – was formed by what

Page | 11

seems like just an incident in history. It was not just a few months of disruption, it cracked their whole being. The ordeal of leaving this lives, and dead family members behind, never left them. Any images from Partition records make Tariq terribly fearful of seeing their faces in them. Having always imagined those pictures as past, it strikes him as he was scared to see what he had lived through.

People saw migrating after Partition - Taken from Tariq's personal collection

To that point onwards, violence on the streets of Bharatpur among Hindus and Muslims began to intensify. People moved away from, or were forced out of, mixed areas and took protection in increasingly separated ghettos. The Raja of that time helped the rioters to start the anti-muslim movement. Above one million citizens died in the associated riots and fighting at local levels, mainly in the western region of Punjab which was cut in two by the border. The mutinies were a result of a lack of military and political control on the part of the British who had colonized India. Tariq and his family saw the vilest mutinies of Bharatpur. He recalled men and women being taken away from their houses by the throngs, and trucks full of corpses passing by their house. Neighbors started slaughtering one another and childhood friends became sworn enemies. Along with Muhammad Tariq Khan, 14 million people left their homes in fall of 1947, when the colonial British administrator began dismantling the empire in southern Asia. The heritage of that fierce departure has endured, triggering a bitter rivalry between India and Pakistan. When they separated, there were perhaps no two nations on Earth as alike as India and Pakistan. Cottages and houses were burned and burgled and children were killed in front of their siblings. His father was on duty when rioters attached their house all of a sudden and they had to take refuge in a Masjid. The only safe place left for Muslims was Jama Masjid, so his uncle, who lived there, had come to take them He told them that they didn't have time to pack or think again, so they left in the state they were in. They stayed in the basement of a mosque for one night where they felt terrified by the dark and choked by a large number of people hiding there with them. He remembered when his uncle confirmed the rumors of rioters headed towards their area and advised them to leave everything immediately. They had to escape the house without taking any of their belongings. Tariq still remembers that he didn't even turn down the burning stove, and still remember the flame. After few days of this chaos and bloodshed, they all migrated to Agra. The train carrying refugees among the two nations arrived fully with corpses, all the passenger had been killed. Muhammad Tariq Khan, his family and some of the other refugees from Bharatpur got blessed and reached Agra. Partition triggered mass casualties and a colossal wave of migration. Tariq was six years old when he boarded an overloaded train bound for the newly-created Muslim state of Pakistan,

Muhammad Tariq Khan moved to what they hoped would be safe territory, with Muslims heading towards Pakistan while Hindus and Sikh towards India. Estimations of the death toll after partition was around 2 million. Numerous killed by members of other communities and sometimes their own families, as well as by the infectious diseases which swept through refugee camps. Women were often targeted as symbols of community honor, with up to 100,000 raped or kidnapped. Most of the ferocity was in Punjab and to a slighter degree Bengal, where long-lasting hatred among Hindu majority and Muslim and Sikh minorities urged on by agitated politicians, exploded in the full-scale slaughter. People just changed overnight and on the label of religion, they were prepared to do anything. "Those people who migrated from East Punjab were in a very bad condition. There were many injuries, by the thousands. There were killing and rioting there. But those who were not physically harmed, they were just crazy for opportunities, to acquire property that the Hindus and Sikhs had left behind – jobs, opportunities, properties. There was a big vacuum which translated into material opportunities. And that became the norm, and over seventy years I think it is that norm that has progressed. The norm of acquiring personal benefits, material benefits", Tariq explained.

Muslims before partition were mostly a cultivator's class deprived of economic opportunities of education, jobs, health care, hygiene, and housing," says Tariq. Whatever social opportunities were available were confined to the Hindus and patronized by the British who believed in "divide and rule." It is apparent that Partition helped the social mobility of Muslims of East Bengal. The success story of Tariq's father and their family, typical of many more similar Muslim families, would have remained a far cry, a distant mirage in the absence of Partition.

At that time the recently made governments were totally bare to deal with immigrants of such surprising magnitude, and huge violence and massacre happened on both sides of the border. A makeshift refugee camp was set up on the route to Karachi, Pakistan. The set up was typical for those who traveled on foot for all or some part of their journey. They set up camp using the little belongings they had set off with, mostly on camel carts. In Karachi, they stayed at the refugee camps. Tariq remembers his mother running around in the refugee camp and fetching kerosene oil for three coins to light the lamp and stoves in their tent.

A glimpse of a refugee camp in Karachi- Taken from Tariq's personal collection

After a few months of migration along with the immigrants of Bharatpur, Muhammad Tariq Khan met his father at Karachi port. His father was posted in Rohri Sukkur and they started living there. Their struggles did not end even after migration; it took their family years to find their bearings and settle down in the new nation. But what is exemplary is that his parents never complained about the struggling times and were always thankful for the new nation. And this is not specific to him, hundreds and thousands of families faced similar circumstances but never lost their passion and loyalty to Pakistan.

He left everything behind during partition and hoped for a new life, for land and home. But not everyone was as lucky-they were killed while trying to cross the border to India and Pakistan. Some of the migrants ended up in homes of people who migrated in other direction while others ended up in cities, Muslims in Karachi and Hindus in Calcutta. Tariq believes that the British Army, which was still in India at the time, could have done more to stop the carnage. Tariq's father told him that his grandfather pleaded the British soldiers who were there to end the killing but they said their orders were not to interfere. Seventy years on and many people feel this dark chapter in human history has largely been overlooked. "It was genocide. More than a million people died but it's something people tried to forget happened," says Tariq. "There are no memorials in India or Pakistan and there was never a public inquiry or investigation into what happened. Tariq says it was the media at the time that started spreading hatred among the communities and also several politicians who wanted to stir up people's feelings for their own use. Old differences among Muslims and non-Muslims became highlighted. His village escaped the massacre but he remembers the stressed atmosphere. "A railway line ran through our farm where we lived and I remember seeing the trains full of immigrants. They were sitting on top of the carriages and there were soldiers to protect them from attack." Upon Tariq, his family and arrival of the Muslim refugees in Pakistan – there was no base of accommodation for the immigrants. Again, the leadership had to resort to public buildings and barracks – immigrant and aid camps were set up and the food was given to the refugees.

Late in the 1950s, most of Urdu speaking immigrants who traveled after the independence were settled in the port city of Karachi in southern Sindh and in the urban cities of Hyderabad, Sukkur, Nawabshah, and Mirpurkhas. Furthermore, some of the Urdu speaking people were settled in the cities of Punjab, mostly in Lahore, Bahawalpur, Rawalpindi, and Multan.

Though many Hindus, Sikhs, and Muslims survived in tightly-knit groups prior to the partition, the partition saw extraordinary genocidal violence. Though, Tariq claims that religious violence and spiritual segregation did not exist before the partition. But people co-existed and his family experienced usually peaceful lives living in the other communities. The seeds of Islamophobia were implanted a few years earlier to partition, and extended to a violent leaning point during the partition, as neighbors and friends suddenly turned on each other. Partiality trickled down to the distinct level. The Muslim, Hindu, and Sikh communities dishonored each other, with Hindus and Sikhs standing united against Muslims. The trauma that Tariq has inherited is covered up with patriarchal histories, a wide loss, dreadful hatred, silence, and a complex class and caste status.

Two Nation Theory was the basis of partition. Tariq always appreciated how Jinnah's ideology shaped Pakistan's identity. The Subcontinent – a vast multi-ethnic, multi-religious, multi-racial and multi-class mass of number and a cauldron of huge conflicts – was separated in an exceptionally rushed, inconsiderate, dishonest, expeditious and blood-spattered manner. And it has continued to be divided into social, cultural, philosophical, spiritual/sectarian and terrestrial lines within and between the three states of the Subcontinent. The events which took place in the late 1920s and

1930s led the Muslims to think that maybe their destiny lies in a separate state. This concept developed the demand for partition. Iqbal in his speeches and writing reiterated the claims of Muslims to be considered a nation which is based on race, history, the unity of language, religion, and identity of economic interests. Tariq remembered how his father along with other Muslims played an important role in the uprising against British Authority in 1857, the British were anti-muslim during the early post-uprising period. His father used to tell him about the difficulties which Muslims have faced before and after partition. In 1934, Jinnah returned as a leader of the Muslim League after a period of residency in London but found id divided and without a sense of mission. He set about restoring a sense of purpose to Muslims and emphasized the Two Nations Theory. In the late 1930s, Jinnah was convinced about the need for a unifying issue among Muslims, and Pakistan was the obvious answer. Two Nation Theory's phenomenon basically sprigged up with the arrival of Islam in the Sub-Continent. The sense was very exclusive about Pakistan's creation that it was generally based on moral commitments in the light of Islam. The basic idea behind Two Nation Theory was Muslims and Hindus was two separate nations from each expects.

Childhood

Ast Tariq grew up he was told about the story of how his family came to Pakistan with nothing except the clothes on their backs, time and time again, growing up. Fear, anger, hatred, sadness, and hopelessness accompanied their stories. All of their possessions were on their bodies. Women in my family buried jewelry, money, and other precious items in their homes, thinking they would go back for it. The governments did not allow them to bring any vehicles, machinery or other belongings as this was to belong to the country they left. Though, they probably would not have taken anything with them, since it would have slowed them down. More significantly they did not think that moving to Pakistan would be permanent. This left them in an unfortunate situation as they suddenly plummeted down the class ladder. They lost the deed to their lands and were never given any appropriate compensations. They thought that they were escaping the violence and that they would return to their homes when normality was restored, but the new normal held no space for them. This search for home, of belonging, is in his blood.

A rare picture from Tariq's personal collection, Muslims sitting on the top of the train near New Delhi

During their journey to Karachi, Muhammad Tariq Khan was grieving. He was five years old and was terrified to leave the only life he knew. He had heard of Pakistan but did not know where it was, what it would be like, or what would he do there. He recalls it was a very hard time for his family. They had very little land, and his father Abdul Hameed Khan was a very honest man. They confronted many hurdles. Before the partition, Tariq had a very happy childhood in Bharatpur. It was a Hindu area, so as Muslims they couldn't leave the house. Their neighbors were Sikh and they had said they would protect them, but that didn't happen. He counts himself as fortunate because of the stories he heard about the children being killed by Indians in horrific ways. He recalled that as a five-year-old, he was scared and captivated by the ferocity. They weren't allowed to go out much. But they would race out every opportunity they got because every day they found chopped heads on the road.

Tariq also explained the problems faced by Pakistan after partition as, "Pakistan from its very start tackled a large number of problems like; parting of borders, relocating of Muslims in Punjab, Immigrants' resettlement, the agreement of Hyderabad, Junagadh, and Kashmir, Division of Indian Assets, Administration Problems, Language Controversy, and Population Difficulties. Several encounters in setting up new financial, legal, and political structures, establishing the government and the armed forces, resettle the Mohajir (Muslim immigrants from India), and start the circulation and balance of power in the local and central governments were standing ahead. Pakistan was in such a struggling situation, though Quaid was in ill health, he tried hard to keep the end up. He powerfully took the hold of the state and international affairs. His policies to run Pakistan in the post-partition era had a close link to that of the strategies to establish Pakistan".

Being born in a Muslim family, Muhammad Tariq Khan was taught about the oneness of Allah and his messenger Prophet Mohammad (Peace Be Upon Him). At the age of five, he started learning Holy Quran and memorized some part of it. The place he lived was comprised of 60% Hindus, 15% Christians and only 15% of the Muslim population. He used to play with the neighborhood boys every day and it was fun. He remembered his father telling his stories about how Muslims were suffering in India. The partition memories, the disgust and cruelty of the time, the harkening back to a—often mythical—past where Hindus and Muslims and Sikhs survived together in comparative peace and coherence, have shaped the staple of stories Tariq have lived with.

Normally children love either love to read, draw or play on their own, but Muhammad Tariq Khan was equally interested in education and sports. When he migrated to Pakistan, he had a huge passion for sports and competition. He played several different sports like badminton while growing up. There was something he always loved about working hard, competing and getting better day by day. His parents also encouraged him to play several different sports as a young child. To them, winning was not as important as trying your best and displaying a good sportsmanship. Playing sports with these values and goals, rather than the pressure to win, grew his respect and love for sports and he began to spend a lot of time playing them.

At the time of partition, Karachi suffered the widespread outbreaks of community violence among Muslims and Hindus, who were the target of Muslim refugees coming from India. The refugees who left their belongings, houses and some of them even their relatives in a search of a better living in Pakistan have faced discrimination here as well.

Karachi at the time of independence was chosen as the capital of Pakistan. The city experienced a decline as a result of partition because most of the business was controlled by Hindus and Sikhs. Karachi became the capital of Pakistan in August 1947. It observed a huge influx of Muslim immigrants arriving from several Indian cities and towns. Karachi did not have the assets to accommodate such an arrival. Several of its buildings were packed to capacity. Many civil servants, police personnel and ministers of the new country shifted to these tents from where (for almost a year and a half) they steered the fate of Pakistan and its capital city. They reached Lahore at dawn. It was an instant of great relief. Locals greeted them at the train station and fed them during a six-hour stay before they continued their journey to Karachi. Some of the people on the train with Tariq and his family were already victims of communal violence. He realized that something horrible was going to happen. Finally, the train moved on and he saw dead bodies everywhere. He turned pale. It was the first time he saw deaths on such a scale.

The day Pakistan came into existence, it typically contained economically recessive and weak areas. The agricultural system was invalid and obsolete which added to the financial backwardness of the areas creating part of Pakistan. Before partition, the Hindus, with the permissions of the British Government, had established complete domination in trade and commerce. The whole capital was in the hands of the Hindus. Unluckily, the banks and other financial institutes were located in Indian Territory. The main industries were also in those parts which were the portion of India.

The city of Karachi was the home to 350,000 people before partition; about 125,000 of those were Hindus or Parsi who left for India. In return, 500-600,000 Muslim immigrants had flooded into the city. When Tariq and his family reached, Karachi was an over-crowded city with individuals sleeping on paths with all of their insufficient possessions — little bundles that stood near them. Some did not rise in the morning and were dragged away.

Muhammad Tariq Khan's journey to Karachi was troubled with challenges and struggles. Individuals often went starving for days and diseases were widespread. The riots and ferocity that they suffered just made it all the more hard. Trains would often arrive filled with only the dead bodies of the passengers. When Tariq and his family landed on Karachi port, the city seemed welcoming and familiar. The leftovers of the vicious communal riots were still very much in evidence. Karachi was a sea of immigrant camps when they reached. Soon, they were taken to Rohri Sukkur where his father was posted. Whatever happened in 1947, particularly during the train journey, is deeply engraved in his memory. The murderous faces of the Sikh mobs shaped the most unforgettable moment of his life. Traveling to Pakistan appeared like the mere option for Muslims. From being second-class people in India they suddenly had a motherland of their own. In the initial days, there was intense pain, misunderstanding, resentment, and fear – but all that was hustled up and pushed aside to focus on preparing and working towards a better future.

A picture was taken on the port when Tariq and his family arrived in Karachi – Personal Collection

Tariq and his family migrated in the faith of a better future and thought about living with their own people. But it was nothing more than a mere paradise. The native of Pakistan also treated them as second-class citizens, as burdens on their society. Tariq began to understand that Partition was certainly more than just a political divide, or a partition of properties, of assets and liabilities. It was also, to use a saying that survivors use frequently, a `partition of hearts. It carried indescribable sorrow, disaster, shock, agony, and ferocity to societies who had previously lived together in a certain kind of community contract. It parted families across a randomly drawn boundary, occasionally overnight, and made it almost impossible for individuals to know if their parents, sisters, brothers or children were living or dead. His life has always been shaped by the partition, so researching the partition is of utmost relevance to him as it not only explores the history of his family but of thousands of families that were forced to flee their homes.

Mesmerizing view of Rohri Bridge over River Indus captured by Tariq

Tariq and his family started living on a small hill near Lansdowne Rohri Sukkur which is a 19th-century bridge that spans the Indus River among the cities of Rohri and Sukkur, in Sindh province. It is a city of the largest man-made monuments and the most significant among them is Lansdowne Bridge and Ayub Arch. This bridge was the only way to connect Rohri to Sukkur and is located on River Indus. The beauty of this bridge attracts the locals walking around the bridge. It was a beautiful view from his home and he also spent time enjoying the beauty of the River Indus and breathtaking fresh air, Life seemed closer to recovery from the setbacks they had suffered.

Family Life

Karachi proved to be more prosperous for Tariq and his family. His father has prospered much by this time. Tariq's father name was Abdul Hameed Khan and mother was Akhtari Begum. Tariq was the second among his sisters and brothers. He had four brothers: Muhammad Tahir Khan, Shakir Abdullah, Gulam Abdul Qadir Jillani, Muhammad Sadiq and three sisters: Mubeen Fatima, Momna Khatoon, Shahnaz Fatima.

Tariq with his wife Parveen and children: Shazia, Fouzia, and Shariq, Atif and Saquib – Photo Studio at Cairo, Egypt

His mother was a religious and hardworking woman. India was a multicultural society where faiths and beliefs regulate the life of an individual. It was not easy for her to protect her children from the Indians. There was a difference between the cultural diversity which included attitudes, habits, languages, and traditions. Tariq's mother died in the year 1968, because of the age factor. His mother was his first friend and playmate. No one ever told him about the pain he would feel from losing his mother. Losing a parent was a very emotional time for Tariq and his family. It was a very difficult time for Tariq to deal with the loss of his mother. Speaking about his mother death Tariq says, "Grief is a hole, endless and vast. Sucking you dry of any emotions you might think you have. When my mother died I felt trapped, alone and helpless most of the times than I ever thought I would be in my whole life. I was drowning in grief, unable to see a light out". Tariq was only 26 years old when his mother died. He found his mother lying unresponsive in the living room of their home. She was slumped in her favorite chair with a very peaceful expression on her face, her eyes were closed as if she was dreaming about some glorious land. She passed away peacefully in her sleep from natural causes. That night, Tariq remembered telling his best friend, between sobs on the phone: "She won't see me turn 30". Adults are often surprised at the emotions which can intimidate to overwhelm them following the death of a parent. After all, the reason, it is in the natural order of things that children will one day bury their parents.

Throughout most of his 20s, Tariq believed that he had experienced many of the joys and troubles of a young adult. He graduated from college, started playing badminton, developing a relationship with parents, grew out friendships and so much more. He imagined it a breeze turning to 30s, has garnered a wealth of knowledge and wisdom through the trials of his 20s. Little did he know he was about to face the most difficult challenges of his life. He never thought his mother would leave him at an early age. He dreamt that his parents would grow old together. He could picture them spending weekends with his future kids, recounting stories of when he was young and loved to play badminton. Parents are the pillars of a family unit and this was particularly true for Tariq. After the year since her death, Tariq has learned a great deal about grief. He has learned that it's far more complex than he thought, and not a step-by-step process. Being in the emerging stage when a parent dies can cause young adults to feel like their world has blown up. Same was the case with Tariq when his mother left this world. As he approached 30, it was very difficult reaching a milestone age without his mother physically by his side. Her sage words guided and steered Tariq for the rest of his life. She imparted lessons during and at the surprise conclusions of all his crazy adventures.

"Grief turns out to be a place none of us know until we reach it. We anticipate that someone close to us could die, but we do not look beyond the few days or weeks that immediately follow such an imagined death. We misconstrue the nature of even those few days or weeks. We might expect if the death is sudden to feel shocked. We do not expect this shock to be obliterated, dislocating to both body and mind," says Tariq.

After the death of his mother, his father also died on 20th August 1971. He died suddenly and unexpectedly. Prior to this, the only person in his life who had passed away who he felt remotely close to was his mother. When his dad died, he felt as though he either hadn't seen or hadn't paid attention to many accounts of grieving the death both the parent in your 20s.

After a few days of hardly sleeping and eating and bursting into tears at the slightest remembrance, Tariq asked himself, "When does this end? When can I feel okay again?" I fooled myself into thinking that if I went through the steps if I followed the stages, I would come out on the other end".

"Grief is not unlike being lost out at sea; waves of different emotions continuously crash over you and you feel as if the current will sweep you out even farther from what you once thought was normal. Grief sometimes manifests itself into something a lot darker. Sometimes it turns into something that makes you feel emotions you are unfamiliar and uncomfortable with, and the normal stages of grief can manifest into depression", says Tariq. There's nothing like death to make a person realize how short life is and to get you thinking about the future. Due to this recognition, Tariq brought himself back from the trauma of losing his parents and focused on his future. He focused all of his thoughts towards badminton. This was the turning point in Tariq's life and he created a healing method for himself. He worked through feeling by placing his focus and energy on badminton to overcome anxiety and fear. After losing both parents at 29, Tariq also learned that life is stronger than death, and the love of someone so cherished will always live on. Life went on and in time the pain lessened and I found new things to be grateful for. He learned he was stronger than he first thought.

He further explained the time when he lost his parents, "The death of a parent can create feelings of weakness. When a parent dies, there are often other feelings of loss. There might be the loss of a home, the sense of loss of our link with the past, even the loss of the hope that someday our relationship might have changed. Also, there might be strong feelings of longing – a need to have a parent around 'forever' to share our future accomplishments and offer support in our times of need. There might be regrets – of things said or not said e.g. if only I had said: "I love you".

Loss and struggle hold the seeds of transformation. But as Tariq experienced loss and struggle in his life, he had noticed a pattern: he got stronger, and the seeds of that struggle resulted in his growth and made him a Badminton Champion. Life is a constant process of struggle, transformation, and development. Though, it might not always seem obvious, if you look at growth you can always trace it back to the struggle that preceded it

Tariq's father was a very kind and a generous man. My father was the kindest man I've ever seen, he understood anyone, and he loved all his children equally, says Tariq. Tariq's father was like a true friend. He received so much love and affection from him. His father was a hardworking and a disciplined man. Tariq always looked up to him for advice and his guidance. He taught him the life lesson with much love and patience. Even when Tariq was slow to learn and understand he never lost his temper. Instead, he taught him patiently until he was able to understand.

"My mother and father have been wonderful parents to me. They have worked hard to provide a stable foundation for my life and future. They have taught me invaluable lessons about work, marriage, parenting, relationships, and life, says Tariq. Tariq's parents never found it necessary to mold him into anything that they wanted him to be. Aside from wanting him to grow into an intelligent, kind-hearted person, his parents let him be who he wanted to be. His parents always taught him to speak the truth, because it was the first step that took Tariq towards success. His father always taught him to respect his elders and love those who are younger. His parents taught him to be independent and to have his own opinions and thoughts. Instead of going along with everyone else, or following the popular idea, they taught him to think for himself.

Speaking about his father, Tariq says, "The biggest misconception about being a father is that you have to be tough. I think you have to be soft when it requires it. Most men can be tough when the time requires, but like be soft knowing that they get better results so that it requires a different sort of understanding". Tariq's father never lets him quit the sport. I learned to never quit something because it bores me or is too hard, and I really think it has paid off for me. Not just with physical activities, but my relationships, education, and career as well, says Tariq. From his father, he learned the importance of hard work and education. His father always emphasized that education would be the way to become successful in life. He also emphasized that education would not just bring financial success, but also help to grow as individuals and become independent. He taught him to dream without limits and with ambition. Those were things his father always made sure he emphasized regularly. He taught all of them the true meaning of hard work and the importance of family by the way he walked and talked. Out of so many lessons and ideals, Tariq's dad has taught him throughout his life, the one lesson that is the most important is the value of integrity. His father valued integrity more than anything in a person. He always told Tariq that in order to be successful you must always remain honest. For the minute you lie, all your integrity is gone and you can never be seen in the same light as you once were. "Always do the right thing, even if it's the hardest thing to do," he told Tariq. "In the end, what truly matters is the value of your character and that character should always be honest, genuine, and sincere", says Tariq.

Speaking about his favorite memory with his mother Tariq says, "My mother was the leader of the house. She led every one of us to be able to do everything and she succeeded. What my mother gave me was an example of how a person should live his life by giving unconditional love. From helping us take first baby steps to tell fascinating stories, she's played an important role in our lives. Sometimes the most memorable moments in our childhoods are the small everyday occurrences that contribute to our feeling that all is right with the world. I had many of those with my mother. In an era of stay-at-home-mothers and 'father-knows-best', what I remember most about my mother was that she was always there. When I came down for breakfast – she was there. When I came home from school – she was there. And when I closed my eyes at night - she was there - reading me a bedtime story. My mother was the backbone of our family. No matter the need, she was always there and willing to help. Saying words like love, sacrifice, hard-working, determined, inspiring, responsible, dedicated, supportive, strong and faithful are honorable, but having a mother that demonstrated all these characteristics is priceless. She taught me as a little boy that being helpful, loving, and kind was what was most important. I have found that this advice has not only helped me find happiness and balance in my life but has also helped me to teach my kids the same principles. I knew that I can look up to my mother's advice for support in any task. She was my biggest fan as an adult and always encouraged me to be the best that I can be. Her encouragement was the reason I worked her and made her proud. Whenever I messed up, she picked me back up again. She always had the right words to say and knew when someone needs a word of encouragement. She was very honest and full of integrity. Although she faced hard times in her entire life, she became a better person through it all. My mother was a strong-willed and determined woman and she never let herself or our family down".

A glimpse of Parveen, Tariq's wife in a bridal dress in her marriage ceremonial.

Muhammad Tariq Khan married a girl named Parveen with the consent of his parents. Their wedding took place in the final years of British rule in India. The; newspapers were already reporting on the prospect of a Partition, and there were loud processions on the streets. They both were introduced to each other by their parents as they were to be tied into a sacred knot of marriage. Tariq was married to one of his relatives. Parveen was the daughter of Kazim Hussain who was the close friend of Tariq's uncle Molana Fazlul-Rehman, At the time of marriage Parveen was 18 years old, however, Tariq was of 26 years. Parveen had never met her husband, Tariq but had caught a glimpse of him before the wedding. The festivities lasted for one month because of the long journey on elephants.

Tariq with his wife and children: Shazia, Fouzia, Mustafa, Shariq, Atif, and Saquib - Taken at Photo Studio in Karachi, Pakistan

Tariq and his wife Parveen, both led a very happy, fulfilled and peaceful life and gave birth of six children, including four sons named Mustafa, Muhammad Shariq, Muhammad Atif, and Muhammad Saquib and two daughters named Shazia and Fouzia. All the children of Muhammad Tariq Khan have earned Master's Degree in their respective fields. His elder son Mustafa is married to Tehreem. They have two beautiful daughters named Amna and Ayesha. His daughter Shazia is a married relationship with Syed Faheem Uddin and they have three children names Hammad, Tooba and Faria. Tariq's younger daughter Fouzia is married to Zahir and they have one daughter named Laiba. Muhammad Shariq is married to Maria Bano and both are living a happy and fulfilled life. Atif and Saquib are younger than Shariq and both are also good badminton players with their unique skill sets. Both the younger sons of Tariq, Atif and Saquib are talented and gifted. Tariq has always recognized his son's efforts and supported them throughout their careers.

All of Tariq's sons are living happily because of the values he taught them and raised them to respect others. Kindness, honesty, generosity, self-discipline, compassion, and courage are the values Tariq had instilled in his children. He had protected his children from the potentially negative societal influences and laid the foundation for them to become good citizens. As a parent, Tariq has fulfilled his responsibilities.

Being a grandparent is the best time of my life, says Tariq. He is proud and he knows about the great things which come along with this. There's something incredible about witnessing and seeing your family grow and grow. As a grandparent, Tariq can stand back and watch the future unfold in front of him. As your grandchildren enter the world, it's thrilling to watch them grow, seeing which relatives they might resemble and discovering what type of people they will become as individuals. Noticing the similarities between your own children and their children is a particularly enjoyable aspect.

A rare picture of Tariq's marriage ceremony

Soon after the marriage, they both grew to love each other. His wife was really passionate about whatever she pursues, His wife worked as a teacher for almost 40 years. Being a teacher was the childhood ambition of Parveen. When she was young she always wanted to teach people around her and play her play in uplifting the society. She wanted to become a teacher so that she can have a positive impact on our children. To her teaching was the best she can do. English was always her favorite subject. She was always told by her parents that teaching was a sacred profession and it can make the world a better place.

Tariq with his wife and eldest son Mustafa Tariq at their house – Korangi, Karachi

Arranged marriages are the cultural norms for most of the Muslims around the world. Tariq was also a humble, kind-hearted and passionate person. By praising what you do and not demeaning your ideas or vision, a great woman can stroke your ego and give you the confidence you need to succeed, says Tariq. His wife was a very supportive woman and it's because of her devotion and support that Tariq succeeded in his life. Successful people are often depicted as being exclusively responsible for their success. However, when looking at their promotions, financial compensation status, and career success, it is the spouse that might be applying a bigger influence on that success. Same was the case with Tariq as his wife helped him throughout his career.

Mr. and Mrs. Tariq at their house – Al Falah Society Karachi

As a successful married couple, Tariq and his wife learned to intentionally do things that will bring happiness back when life pulls it away. They both celebrated the good times together and possessed higher levels of commitment, trust, and relationship satisfaction. Tariq's wife always took pride in his accomplishments and improved the health of their marriage. In Tariq's view marriage is not successful only by taking responsibilities but taking care of each other's feelings. Doing something that makes your partner happy, and by doing so, marriage can be made successful.

Mr. Ansari with Badminton Champions, Rohri

While living in Rohri, he started playing badminton when he was about eight in Rohri Nishat Club. Small kids like him were first headed towards the court, began to clear it and then started playing. Tariq continued playing there even at night and started polishing his skills in badminton. The strict discipline and even sleeping habits at home confirmed that Tariq was the first to hit the practice courts at 5:30 AM. This was a half hour prior than his team comrades, ensuring he got some extra court time. Similarly, when practice would get over, his keenness to surpass would lead to him to ask for and then do more physical exercises. In a small club, trying as hard as he could to beat his fellows- it wasn't long before he succeeded. It was a much-demanded game for Tariq both physically and technically, with several years of preparation and obligation required to reach the upper levels of the sport.

Some people get involved in sports to have fun or stay healthy. But for Tariq, badminton was constant. At a time when he couldn't hold the racket – he stood helplessly by the margins of the court and just watched in awe his siblings and his father playing a game and keeping up with the score and watching how tense and exhilarating it was at the same time. This experience of him standing on the margins tested his patience, He was so furious at himself and his little body for not being able to play badminton. Though, years later he got so good that he won almost every game of badminton that he played with almost anyone, including his siblings and his father.

Not only Tariq played badminton, his whole family was interested in playing. It became the symbol of his family and they were famous as Six Brothers in the whole province. It is something that Tariq will never forget. The biggest thing for Tariq is that he was able to make his family proud. He was able to score the goals for his team and for Pakistan. My two brothers, Shakir Abdullah and Abdul Qadir Jillani were also versed players. We laughed at badminton, even though winning a tournament game requires a lethal patience and the kill-stroke ferocity of a mongoose attacking a cobra. You can see the truth of this in matches we played, says Tariq. Tariq's three cousin brothers; Khaliq-Ur-Rehman, Ateeq-Ur-Rehman and Badar-Ur-Rehman were also great players. After the death of Badar Ur Rehman, Farooq Uz Zaman (famous as Peter) took his place. This is what we are Six Brother, says Tariq. Tariq's brother Shakir Abdullah

was also an intelligent player, and fearless," "He learned very quickly and didn't choke on the court." Shakir's attacking style of play-his round-the-head, deep, well-placed, fast smashes, sometimes struck at over 400 kmph, were lethal-combined with his cool on-court behavior made him a delight to watch, says Tariq. Playing badminton was all about moving fast, the rational, reflexes, footwork. Such speed leaves almost no margin for mistake. If you get confused for even a minute, you lose.

You might have a lot of people in your life. There's your younger brother who is always the center of attention and the elder one who always keeps on advising. Sometimes, the really get on your nerves but we are grateful to be surrounded by them, says Tariq. His brothers always looked out for him. Together they went on all sorts of adventures and talked about the things they were passionate about. They messed with each other whenever they got the chance. It's all meant in good fun, and you're excited to see what else is in store. Maybe the bond between brothers has fewer words, fewer obvious sentiments. It's sometimes hard to find amid the loud chaos of childhood, but I think that's exactly what makes it so beautiful. It's sacred, unspoken — trust in the deepest sense of the word, says Tariq.

Abdul Qadir Jillani, Tariq's second brother was also a very versed badminton player. He was always cautious while playing and always wait for his opponent to make a mistake. Qadir's style worked best against an attacking player who lacks consistency, says Tariq. He led consistency for a long time period in his games. Tariq once watches his brother's game before heading for his on pre-match warm-ups. The difference in the brothers' mentality and how it played out in the court was most apparent whenever they played together. Qadir possessed a versatile and dependable backhand. He was able to execute different shorts with his backhand to keep his opponents honest. Talking about his brother's exceptional qualities Tariq said, "No matter how good a player's footwork is or how strong his around-the-head shot maybe, he cannot compensate for a poor backhand.

Over the years, Tariq has seen his brothers enjoy successful playing careers. Even though one of his cousin brother Khaliq-ur-Rehman garnered more fame than the others in some cases, others are still known among famous badminton players. Tariq was always a fan of his brother, Khaliq-ur-Rehman. He never minds following the footstep of his brothers. In fact, that's how he guided his life and his results on the badminton court just depict that. Khaliq –Ur-Rehman was best in his footwork and it brought him more success in the game. He knew the tactics to reach the shuttle early while on balance. He was so strong and good at hitting shots from the back court. He was always confident about where his opponent will play the next shot. He knew how to maintain a stable posture and balance, to place more of his body weight on his stronger leg and make it his anchoring foot to the ground. And keep the other foot nimble so that he can stretch and reach the shuttle wherever it goes, Tariq added. He mastered the art of adding jumps to his footwork through which he took his skills to the next level. Jumps were especially useful for smashes as this always gave Khaliq-Ur-Rehman a good angle for attack.

Ateeq-ur-Rehman and Badar-ur-Rehman were also good players. They both were good at using more of an underarm backhand serve so intends to be more of a defensive situation. Badminton is all about making risky decisions. You have tactics in place but you also have to adjust to situations. You might plan out a series of shots in advance and follow them through or try to lead your opponent into a certain position. We always work on set plays and most likely outcomes so you need to be clear-minded.

Everybody assumes that you have to be strong to hit a fast smash but it's more about timing and technique. This is what Farooq-uz-Zaman (Peter), Peter's was good at, says Tariq. His strategy was to use lobs and drops to weaken his opponent's footwork and then dominate the game. While putting constant pressure on his opponent, he easily won points. He was also good at footwork and possessed the extraordinary agility and excellent reflexes. The speed and deception in badminton make it harder to predict shots, thus making you rely on your reflexes. Responding quickly to both finesse and power shots is crucial to being competitive in badminton. Smashes can travel over 200 miles per hour, and a similar looking stroke can make a sharp drop shot, says Tariq.

Tariq eldest son Mustafa was also a great badminton player. To be able to hit shuttles at such high speeds or return them, badminton players need to excel in several areas. Mustafa excelled in his physical, tactical, psychological and technical traits. He played on district level and Gym Khana level and won several titles, awards, and matches. He was an aggressive attacker and preferred a fast-paced game and adored smash shots. His skill set was such that he always kept his opponents guessing. This is the hardest thing to teach a child the willingness to work, the desire to win, the hunger to become a champion, says Tariq. Some people call it the "fighting spirit". I call it the "intensity to want to win". This is the one skill I always wanted my son to learn. There can't be any excuses. The next day after training or games, even if he woke up and feel tired, he had to overcome his fatigue, pain, and any other excuses to continue working. This "intensity" is something you either have or don't have.

Mr. Tariq while receiving Open All Pakistan National Championship winning a trophy from Commissioner Income Tax, Karachi

In his developing years, he struggled to have enough shuttlecocks to play and often he has to control or restrict hitting his favorite jump smash. He walked for miles to college and work and avoid using public transport to save money that was used to buy shuttlecocks. As he started to climb the top echelons of Sukkur Badminton Team, his family smilingly endured a lot of hardships and sacrifices. During tournaments, Tariq would play courageously and attack overtly even against top-ranked players.

Tariq receiving the winning trophy for All Pakistan Open Championship from Commissioner Khairpur Division –Lower Sindh

For a talented player as Tariq, winning was the ultimate aim to show progress. He made history by winning back to back titles and trophies. Tariq's family members and his father recognized well how much he got upset during the initial years of his playing the game, but they never shouted, never stopped him, and of course never pulled their rackets on the ground – by that they all taught him a treasured lesson, that having tolerance and admiration is more vital than winning any game. It took him some time to understand that lesson but it is a valued lesson that he knows will come in handy in many aspects of his life.

For years, he had a tough time learning that lesson, particularly when losing a match of badminton. He was so passionately invested in winning that when he lost a game of badminton, his cheeks would turn red, his body would get cold, and he would even cry at times. He would not talk to his match rival for some time. Finally, he had to get over to play another match with him/her. During this moment of him running wild and crying and stomping his foot on the ground, his father, would come over from the other side of the net, and would hug him and calm him down and would explain that, nobody wins every time and that losing is not bad. Every single time, when he had an episode of losing a match, his father would explain that.

Badminton is no less of a habit in his family. It was a very valuable and yet very cherished one too. Moments were born when this game was played. Significant talks were sometimes discussed in the middle of a fast-paced match. And laughs were overheard all over the court. Badminton started only as a tryout when his father was bored in his office and was thinking of doing something fun with his co-workers. Little did he know, that this sport in the next few years would tie several years with many memories. His father beside several of his associates went to campuses to play the sport in the afternoons, but after a while, people got annoying and they had to play in-house. They bought a net, a few wooden rackets a packet of shuttles. And so started the ages of tradition in Tariq's family. Every time he hit the shuttle with his racket, his patience was kind of tested in a small yet very significant way – He had to wait to hit the shuttle at the perfect time otherwise he would either miss it or would hit at the incorrect angle causing a score to his rival's benefit.

It was a huge risk for immigrants to carry valuables on their person while escaping as it meant higher chances of getting looted and killed. But Tariq's family had succeeded to make it this side of the border with a small stash of jewels, a small sense of security to anchor their lives in a foreign land. Tariq's early days in Rohri were full of struggle and resulted in many disappointments. They suffered a lot and at that time Karachi was like burning hole that has stamped their presence and name in the discussion columns around the world. They were turned into a minority in the country, representing only the white part of the flag and were kindly accommodated. Pakistan gave us the identity of which we were deprived of before partition. They were welcomed in Pakistan with fervor and generosity. After partition, most of the people got settled in Karachi and soon became a part of the Punjabi-dominated ruling elite of the new-born country due to the high rates of education found in people who migrated to Pakistan, their urbane tenor and the required expertise they possessed in running Pakistan's nascent bureaucracy and economy.

In the early days after partition, there was a searing pain, confusion, bitterness, and fear – but all that was bundled up and shoved aside to focus on planning and working towards a better future. Families held together, helping each other. Those already living here opened their doors to immigrants. People who migrated to Pakistan replaced the Hindu communities which had controlled trade, commerce, and banking before the partition. Members of traditional trading

communities began to settle largely in Karachi. The immigrants from Gujarat took over the textile import business from Hindu traders. They soon expanded into textile manufacturing, the production of other consumer goods, banking and insurance. They became not only prominent in trade but also leading industrialists. With their high levels of literacy, political and business acumen and solidarity, immigrants affected fundamental changes in the polity, economy, society, and culture of Pakistan.

Things also turned around for Tariq's family with time when they got settled in Rohri. The wounds of the partition have continued 70 years, however, India has developed as a flourishing pluralist democracy while Pakistan - splitting into two with the withdrawal of the East as Bangladesh in 1971 - and Bangladesh has met with difficulties in preserving democracy. Tariq's mother told him the stories of people discovering the heads of their servants placed on their counters or there was one story about a slaughterer who was cutting up meat for a purchaser and then walked across the street and used the blade to slit the throat of a bystander. He was too young to remember all of this. At that time the racial discrimination among Hindus and Muslims were getting more prominent. The Muslims also differ in their social and financial status which ranges from urban to rural poor class. The Muslims were very strict followers of the doctoring of one God, as dictated by their religion and Quran.

Educational Life – A Turn On

After getting settled in Rohri, Tariq started his early education at the age of six from New Yard School. He studies there till 4th grade and then transferred to Islamia School. After partition, the education system in Pakistan was the heritage of British India. Since independence, most of the policies and plan have been formulated the literacy rate in the country. Due to old customs, traditional mindsets and a lack of education, most of the people in Tariq's village do not send their children to school. Since its freedom, Pakistan has embarked upon a number of rural and agricultural growth programs to increase the production and value of the life of rural people. These plans were, Basic Democracies system, Rural Works Program, Village Aid Program, Integrated Rural Development, Peoples Works Program, Local Govt. and Rural Development etc. But all these programs did not achieve the desired results. Tariq was a brilliant and extraordinary student but he was much interested in sports. He maintained his grades equally high and also excelled in sports activities. He was very fond of playing badminton at a very young age. Moving on to the secondary education, Tariq had received training in life talents to reach their full potential through club activities, such as annual school sports festivals. He completed his Matric from Government High School Rohri. Due to the very low income of his father soon after Matric, Tariq started working in a cement company for six years (1960-1966) to support his family and further education. He used to walk home while returning from the factory in scorching sunlight, Sometimes the temperature went up to 50 degrees. After coming home from work drenched in sweat, he took some time to rest and eat lunch then again walked towards Islamia College for evening classes. Islamic College Sukkur was established is 1956 and is three miles away from Tariq's home. He went to the college through Lansdowne Bridge and after this utmost struggle, he finally graduated 1964.

A beautiful portrait of Tariq as a young man

At that time, all the exams from first to final year were conducted under the supervision of Sindh University Hyderabad. His educational journey was full of ups and downs he was awarded for his educational excellence by Sindh University Hyderabad. After graduation, he came to Karachi and appeared in different interviews and then finally got selected by Pakistan International Airlines in 1967. He saw the job application post of PIA in a newspaper and applied immediately. At night, he traveled through Sukkur express and reached Karachi in the morning. He appeared in the interview the same day and again traveled in Sukkur express towards Rohri because he had to appear in the office at 7 am in the morning.

He was hired for the post of senior account assistant due to his experience. While working with PIA, his passion for badminton never faded. After the duty hours, he often went to KPT hall for playing badminton. Badminton was one the most popular game at that time, especially in Asia. Tariq took the advantage of being tall and lean, but it is essential for success. He possessed incredibly athletic ability and high levels of speed, agility, flexibility, strength and muscular endurance.

Tariq participated in Badminton Championship of Pakistan Gymkhana that was held in 1969 and is receiving a trophy for singles from the chief guest. He was very young at that time but always played with dedication and enthusiasm. The sports officer PIA, Mir Mohammad Hussain at that time refused to provide assistance because he was posted on the seat of accounts. He said that the budget is only for the employees in the sports department. Though Tariq was also a National Badminton Champion title holder and also the Champion of PIA and Civil Aviation Authority. While working with PIA at the post of Senior Accounts Managers, Tariq worked hard and received several achievement awards and appreciation letters from the management. He worked up to the expectations and won the hearts of everyone around him.

Tariq Khan of PIA (payroll section) receiving a singles trophy for playing
Pakistan Gymkhana Badminton Championship held in Karachi (1969)

While working in PIA, he was posted to different places which include Sukkur and Turbat. Tariq's experience with Pakistan International Airline was extraordinary as he acquired so many skills and was committed to excellence. As a leading corporation in Karachi, Tariq believed that it was his responsibility to work for the success of his organization. It Throughout his career at PIA, he was awarded different opportunities for professional, technical and personal development. He was given the chance to visit abroad, travel places along with his job responsibilities. In return, the organization was expecting from him the dedication, integrity, and commitment to become a world-class Airline.

He also visited the World Trade Center which is the landmark of Twin Tower. It was a large complex of seven buildings in Lower Manhattan, New York and it was opened in 1973. Tariq was amused by the architecture of the building which was best known for its iconic, 110-story Twin Towers. This tower was made as a framed tube structure, with columns grouped around the perimeter and in the core. He also visited the Statue of Liberty that was a gift of friendship to the United States from the people of France. It is also recognized as a universal symbol of democracy and freedom. He was always fond of traveling and he was also determined to visit the crown of the Statue of Liberty which was the most rewarding experience of his trip to New York.

Passion for Travelling

Ever since he was a kid, Tariq has always loved the adventure of traveling the unknown, something different and new. He was extremely lucky to continuously feed his passion for traveling while working for PIA. He always loved the excitement of feeling like an explorer discovering new lands. Whenever he traveled he was more spontaneous and don't live for past or future, just at the moment. Travelling seems to give him a near constant adrenaline rush. "Travelling has not only been something that I do, but it's been something that has become a part of me I haven't been all over Europe or every continent but I have had my share of travel," says Tariq. After several years of uninterrupted travel and continuous postings, he became quite addicted to this feeling. Travelling could be a challenge, but for Tariq, it was a fun challenge which he enjoyed while conquering time and time again. The reason Tariq loved traveling was it broaden a person's mind in so many ways. You meet new people, share experiences as people get to see how the world lives.

This isn't a distinctive passion; there are several people across the world which share the similar desire to go about the world traveling. Not everybody does it though and the reasons are varied. Some individuals prefer the comfort of their own home and travel vicariously through others, usually referred to as armchair travel. Some people feel limited by finances, work obligations, family, and fear. Others just seem to come up with a constant stream of

justifications and to me, this means you lack passion. If you really wanted it you would do it. That doesn't mean it is easy but it means that you will eventually find a way to satiate your travel passion," says Tariq.

He also traveled to Buckingham Palace in London, which is recognized as a resident and a working royal palace. The gardens of the palace are famous and often described as "a walled oasis in the middle of London". Tariq enjoyed the eastern part of the palace which is perhaps the most important as it is where the royal family steps out onto the balcony to wave to the crowds. The streets which lead to Buckingham Palace are also famous as they serve as "ceremonial approach" route to the palace. After this, he visited Tower Bridge which is his most favorite place in London. Tower Bridge is in the eastern part of London so it was exciting for Tariq to see a part of London he was not familiar with.

A downward view of London Bridge taken by Tariq - November

This bridge is the famous landmark and is connected with two sidewalks which are constructed so they can resist the horizontal forces from the suspended parts of the bridge. The high-level walkways originally allowed people to move across the Bridge when the bascules were raised to allow ships to pass, but it was found people preferred to wait for them to close rather than climb up so public access was discontinued in 1910. In 1982 they were re-opened as part of the Tower Bridge Exhibition and more recently glass floors were installed, which I enjoyed walking along and looking down onto the Bridge and River Thames from 42 meters above, I went to the Tower Bridge when it was opened on a weekday morning in November and it felt like I had the place to myself. It was drizzling a bit earlier that morning, but the rain stopped when I got there.

After taking rest for some days he again started traveling and this time he visited Big Ben, the clock tower. It was built in 1858 and started on May 31st. He also visited Madame Tussauds Museum in London which is one of the chains of wax museums located all over the world. In this museum, he saw more than 400 life-like replicas of the most recognizable faces in the world, ranging from legends and superstars, historical icons and some religious faces. "The wax museum is divided into several zones. This means that people of the same type of celebrity are housed in the same gallery. So, Madame Tussauds is much organized", says Tariq. He was also posted in Egypt which is probably the world's oldest civilization. Tariq enjoyed much more than just pyramids and monuments, He also visited River Nile and the experienced their culture. He defined Egypt as a land bustling with life, sound, visual beauty and excitement. He also visited their temples and pyramids that have captured the imagination of travelers for thousand years. A rule of their etiquette was that greetings must lead all forms of social collaboration. An individual joining any kind of group, even of outsiders, is expected to meet those already present. In less unknown circumstances shakes are due. Embracing is also common as a method of greeting, typically among members of the similar sex," he told. He was treated with hospitality and was also offered tea as a visitor. The most awe-inspiring temple according to Tariq was the great Sun Temple of King Ramses II at Abu Simbel. The temple was guarded by the four famous colossal statues of the pharaoh. Tariq also spoke about this unbelievable natural marvels provided for a most spectacular sight. He arrived at the sanctuary afore sunrise and witnessed the shafts of light slowly creeping through the rock-hewn inner Hypostyle Hall.

Next visit was to the Pyramids of Giza. On a local bus in Cairo one day, he struck up a conversation with an Egyptian. His English was nearly perfect and, after the typical pleasantries about where he was from, his next question was, what places you want to visit?

Tariq told him about his plan to visit the pyramids of Giza. Tariq took a bus from Midan Tahrir to the pyramids, which is the large public square in the center of Cairo. When he arrived there he took a ride on a camel and negotiated the fee. From there he took a cab to reach the pyramids, the driver agreed on a fair price because he was a local. When he reached there and saw the pyramids, it was no surprise as being one of the Seven Wonders of the World, He also paid some amount to get inside the pyramid. He was expecting a grand entrance into the hollow building where he can look up to the highest point in the middle, but he was greeted by a small opening that led to a narrow tunnel. The tunnel than started to shorten and ascend for several meters before he reached to the Queen's Chamber.

Tariq with his wife Parveen and children, Fouzia, Shazia, Atif and Saquib at the magnificent Pyramid of Giza - Cairo

Tariq with his wife Parveen and children, Shazia, Fouzia, Atif and Saquib at
Pyramids of Giza - Egypt

At the Queen's chamber, the tunnel gets taller and leads for several
more meters higher up into the Great Pyramid. He spent 20 minutes
in the pyramid but could take the picture from inside because
cameras were not allowed. There's no doubting the attractive history
of the several ancient Egyptian worlds and the Pyramids of Giza are
the icons of this past. We had to sometimes pinch ourselves to
understand that we were at this epic wonder of the world. The scale
of these buildings can only be truly appreciated when you are there,
standing in front of them, "says Tariq.

Tariq with his wife at Pyramids of Giza, Egypt

Traveling allowed Tariq and his family to experience new surroundings and forced them to reflect on those passed. It has all the ingredients for making new memories and revisiting old ones. It's about seeing places and sights for the first time and knowing you've done it together. It's about creating memories that you can look back on for years to come, knowing you shared them with each other. Tariq and his wife saw the most impressive sights, ate the best food, but most of all, they met the most incredible people.

After getting done with work requirements and taking rest of some days, Tariq again planned his visit to the Valley of Kings, he had heard about the myths and legends of these placed from numerous people. For visiting the valley he took a rover train which is named as Taftaf and it goes for about 15 kilometers from the Luxor Bridge to the valley, which was located in an arid area between the large hills in the desert. This region has the leftovers of dried waterways that were found here for thousands of years, During the trip, Tariq saw about 64 tombs, that were engraved in the hard rocks, some of them were small while others contain more than 120 room and it was a wonderful scene. In the road throughout the trip to Valley of the Kings, he saw monuments like Colossi of Memnon in the green fields, temples of El-Dier El-Bahari, and the house of Howard Carter, the Egyptologist who discovered the tomb of King Tutankhamen; the age of this house is over 80 years and he lived in it for about 15 years during the excavation works.

On reaching the Valley of Kings, Tariq started his own exploration of the tombs with a little frustration though. Photos weren't allowed anywhere in the valley, in order to stop people from taking cameras down into the tombs themselves. It was a smart policy, and while he was at first a little annoyed he quickly let go of it and relished the ability to throw himself into the experience. "It's nice to put down the camera sometimes and to enjoy the moment for what it is, and the Valley of the Kings is the ideal place to do just that," he added.

When he arrived at the Valley, he found the Visitor Center which contained signs and photos with some information like the reason of choosing this site, explanations of some scenes that what people will find in this tomb. He quoted his explorations as: "The Valley stands on the west bank of the Nile, opposite modern-day Luxor and for more than 500 years among the 16th to 11th centuries BC assisted as the final resting place for the leaders of ancient Egypt. Firmly built in the mid of the desert to deter thieves, most of the tombs were raided in ancient times, but the tombs that stay still offer significant clues to the past. Not all the tombs were raided though; this is where Howard Carter discovered the tomb of Tutankhamun in 1922, complete with its resources and new tombs are still being traced today. It's a place of power where the mind takes over full control and I couldn't wait to see it all with my own eyes. Walkways connect the numerous mounds to each other, their treasures of information just underneath the surface. Every day a few of the tombs were open to visitors and everyone follows a similar trail around the accessible parts of the valley. Next to each mound, open or not, is a sign with the name of the ruler who once rested below.

As he started to walk down the pathway that took him into the bowels of the earth, Tariq couldn't help but think of the original archeologists who re-discovered the Valley. The tombs were dark, today lit of course, but back then must have been threatening and more than a little scary to travel for the first time. But immediately he saw what kept them going, interesting murals seemed on either side, leading him deeper into the tombs – the colors still remarkably clear and as inspiring as when they were first painted. The sun was high on his head as he braced his eyes for the bright light after emerging from the tombs. Walking back to the rover train he looked behind and

shook his head in amazement. He couldn't believe that he was privileged enough to have visited one of the most famous gravesites in the world. It was once in a lifetime experience for him. During his tenure in Egypt, he was posted in Cairo from Pakistan International Airport as a finance manager for four years. At that time the President of Pakistan, Rafique Tadar also came to the Cairo for a visit before his retirement. The President appreciated the services of Tariq for PIA and his achievements during his sports career. He honored the journey of Tariq in becoming the most successful badminton player of his time and one of the most inspiring personality in PIA. He also appreciated how Tariq has shown high levels of development in his professional career and in different national events. Speaking at Tariq, the President said that he is an asset of the airline and is the front line representatives of the airline both in Pakistan as well as abroad. He congratulated Tariq for being a Badminton Champion and emphasized on the need to continue with the same zeal and passion which he said are bringing in positive results for the airline.

After his retirement, the newly appointed President Pervez Musharraf also came to Cairo. Tariq along with Ambassador of Pakistan, Mr. Tayabi, Nur-Ullah Khan and Mansoor Alam came to the airport for President's welcome. President Musharraf also honored Tariq's **s** lifetime contribution made to develop and promote the game of badminton. He praised him for his exceptional career as a badminton player and his achievements. He honored Tariq about he contributed immensely to the sport and PIA, and the leadership that Tariq has provided and that his entire team provides contributes to the safety and security of the Pakistani people. On that day and every day, Tariq is truly grateful for his leadership and his services for Pakistan. He also recognized Tariq's extraordinary work in providing better services to the Pakistan airline and working extra with high-efficiency for the betterment of the airline.

Tariq with Mr. Tayyab (Excellency Ambassador), Noor Ulla Khan (Deputy Ambassador)
in Pakistan Embassy – Cairo, Egypt

At that time, almost three Ambassadors were changed with the gap of one year. He always used to go to the Pakistan Embassy for Eid festivities. Particularly for the welcome party of newly appointed Ambassador. After some time Nur-Ullah Khan was posted to UAE. Tariq had developed close family ties with the Ambassador Nur-Ullah Khan. After being posted in UAE, the Ambassador remembered Tariq Khan and sent him a visit visa. He also appointed Tariq's daughter Shazia in Abu Dhabi as a teacher, but she couldn't join because of some personal issues.

Tariq with Pakistan Military Commander (ADC) and Tariq Niazi (Hockey Olympian) at Pakistan Embassy –Cairo, Egypt.

At the time when Tariq was posted in Cairo, the city was a fascinating window into the modern Middle East, the heart of the Islamic world for 1,400 years. It was a huge, vibrant city, the largest and liveliest city in Africa and the Middle East, with between 16 and 20 million residents. During the years Tariq has met dozens of people and famous personalities who have made comfortable lives for him and others in Cairo. One positive thing about living in Cairo it is that you do feel like you are living in a city. Living near the Nile gave us breathtaking views but also a symphony of cars and boats crossing the river all night long, says Tariq.

Tariq's visit to the University of Cairo with his wife Parveen and children, Shazia,
Fouzia, Mustafa, Atif and Saquib

Tariq also visited Cairo University with his wife and children. Cairo University occupies a huge batch of ground overseeing the River Nile. A great part of it is situated in Cairo Governorate, while another part of it and the General Administration of Cairo University are situated in Giza Governorate. This university is one of the oldest, biggest and most famous University in not only in Egypt but also in Africa and the Middle East. Cairo University, a comprehensive institution of higher learning located in Giza,

Egypt, is committed to preparing students for the challenges of a rapidly changing workplace. University's main campus contains 27 faculties and institutes. The entire university has around 300,000 students including 15,000 international students.

During his stay in Cairo, he also met the spiritual leader of the Dawoodi Bohri Community, Sayed Burhan Uddin. He was the leader of the Dawoodi community after succeeding his father Syed Taher Saifuddin in 1965. Tariq met him in the year 1998, later he died in the year 2014 at the age of 102. Each year, several families went to Cairo for a spiritual journey, where they took part in pilgrimages at various places such as the Rasul Hussain with their spiritual leader Syed Burhan Uddin. He was very inspired of his personality as under the leadership of Sayed Burhan Uddin, the Bohri community achieved remarkable social, economic and educational success across the globe. He was known as the ambassador of peace and goodwill and was highly respected by the leaders and governments of the world for his endeavors in promoting international harmony and brotherhood. Among his main offerings was to control and support to the community's knowledge efforts through 400 educational institutions in the world to impart spiritual, divine and secular education.

The Syed Burhan Uddin exhorted his followers to conduct businesses joining merchant and Islamic principles. With a view to nurturing healthy businesses, he established the concept of the Quran for interest-free loans. Tariq was very impressed by his teachings and efforts he made during his lifetime. He strongly believed in giving back to nature through environmental conservation programs and stopping environmental degradation, says Tariq. On the social front, Syed Burhan Uddin encouraged and institutionalized the tradition of mass marriages to curb wasteful spending on luxurious marriage. To see the developments of his followers personally, he traveled far and wide to the lands. He also guided them practically in all aspect of their life including challenges faced in different vicinities and situations. His constant and strong attention to the adherence to their faith, while being law-abiding citizens earned the community immense respect and recognition everywhere in the world.

He was also honored with the highest civilian title like the Star of Jordan and Order of Nile by the respective government of Jordan and Egypt. He was also conferred as an Honorary Doctorates for his efforts in the developing social and educational growth by renowned institutes like Al-Azhar University Cairo, Aligarh Muslim University and the University of Karachi, says Tariq. Burhan Uddin's death was followed by a series of sympathies from several Pakistani political leaders as the local Bohri community grieved the death of their divine leader.

Speaking about Syed Burhan Uddin's educational contributions, Tariq explained, "Among the several educational programs initiated by Syed Burhan Uddin, the Attalim initiative is the most far-reaching for the moral and religious education of children. It has around 700 centers in the different place occupied by the Bohri community all over the world. He always encouraged, endorsed and supported, and personally oversaw the administration of all the education centers. Among the educational efforts of Sayed Burhan Uddin, the prime was the 200 years old Arabic Academy. The Academy continues to remain the mainstay the Bohri community's learning tradition. Initially, this academy was known as Dars-e-Saifee. Syed Burhan Uddin established a second campus in Karachi, Pakistan in 1983, the third one in Nairobi and Kenya. The fourth campus was set up in Marol, Mumbai. All of these institutes offer modern educational services such as laboratories for empirical sciences, computers and languages and voluminous libraries renowned for housing some of the greatest Islamic archives in the world.

Tariq was also fond of the Egyptian music that was a mixture of indigenous, Mediterranean, African and Western elements. He saw those playing harps and flutes which also included two indigenous instruments, ney, and oud. He was also influenced by the Egyptian pop music that has become increasingly important in Egyptian culture while folk music was played during festivities. He lived in Cairo for more than four years and was excited during his time in Cairo. After a four hour flight to Cairo, bit unpleasant with the flight and the squalling kids who never shut up. During this trip, Tariq spent almost a month in Egypt visiting Cairo, Luxor, Aswan, Abu Simbel, the Red Sea and Alexandria. He visited Nile Cruise so many times and also with President Musharraf. There is no better way to explore the Great Pyramids than on a small boat down to the Nile River. The

Nile was the lifeblood of Egypt and Muhammad Tariq Khan could not just miss it. Without seeing this amazing river it was unlikely that the ancient civilizations which make Egypt so popular today would have even existed. He mostly visited the Nile during the months between October and April because during these months the average temperature of 20 degree keeps the things cool, dry and comfortable. Historically, the easiest way to travel through Egypt, the Nile Cruises have been carrying visitors between Luxor and Aswan for over a century. Nile Cruise also offers the magnificent entertainment programs which include visits to the most famous historical monuments of Luxor and Aswan. During his visit, Muhammad Tariq Khan explored the most attractive places in Aswan and Luxor which include High Dam, Temple of Philae and the Valley of Kings. Muhammad Tariq Khan, during his visit, enjoyed the winding along the river at a very relaxed pace. Every morning he woke up and went to visit temples or tombs, usually in small groups along with a guide. He found it very interesting to learn about the Ancient Egyptians generally built temples along the east bank of Nile and tombs along the west. After that morning tour, he returned to his boat for lunch. He visited other sites in the afternoon and spent the river by enjoying the sights and sounds of the river. He always enjoyed sitting on the open deck, seeing the fisherman float past on their feluccas. The ships of Nile Cruise have wonderful facilities and the services of high standards. The River Nile has a personality all of its own. The sleepy, slowly flowing waters are serene in the extreme, and it's a strangely hypnotic experience to sail down the river, observing the fishermen (many still using traditional methods to catch fish, quiet little villages, and of course, the crumbling temples that line the muddy river banks, says Tariq.

During his visits, he also went to the temple of Horus in Edfu, which is located 60km to the north side of Aswan. As our ship floated into the docking area, the warmth of the sun during early morning promised another beautiful day. After the breakfast on board the Nile Cruise, we were ready to visit the Temple of Horus in Edfu. Edfu is a small city in which around 60,000 people lived at that time which is located near Aswan on the Nile River. From the top deck of the cruise, I could clearly see men sitting in a café by the roadside. As the ship pulled up beside the Nile, there came the caleche drivers and made a queue by the gate of the dock, says Tariq. He was delighted by taking one of the caleches to visit the temple. This temple was built between 237 and 57 BC, and it's the best-preserved monument in Egypt. It is preserved by the desert sand, this is the most atmospheric ancient building. Some of the main highlights at the temple include the countless inscriptions visible on its walls, as well as the inscriptions and reliefs that adorn the entrance to the temple which is by way of a massive pylon measuring 36 meters high. The pylon itself is also decorated with various reliefs, or sculptures depicting Ptolemy XII conquering his enemies. Also, the two twin granite larger than life falcons guarding the gateway to the temple is really a sight to behold, says Tariq.

Mr. Tariq with his wife Parveen and children, Shazia, Fouzia, Shariq and Atif
during an evening in Cairo- Egypt

Tariq also visited lee Pacha Nile Cruise Hotel, with his family. It was the right place for us to go as we were looking for an extravagant Nile side dining, say Tariq. Le Pacha Cruise featured nine restaurants that offered scrumptious meals from around the world. It was the best restaurant in Egypt. The venue of this hotel was located in the upscale Zamalek area. Muhammad Tariq Khan and his family enjoyed cuisine from China, Japan, Thailand, and India. This restaurant was among the best for evening dining. This hotel was the essence of Egypt's ancient taste and modern style brought together with experience. It was the landmark of Cairo dining and entertainment venues. Moored along the bank of river Nile along the Island of Gezira, this boat features restaurants and rooms which offer international cuisines and a spectacular view of Nile. I had lunch there with my family and it was great. The food was great; the taste, cleanses, and the variety. The staff is very professional and friendly, says Tariq.

Tariq with his wife Parveen and children, Mustafa, Shazia, Fouzia, Shariq, Atif, Saquib Khalili Bazar, Cairo

This was independent travel, arranging transport and accommodation as he went on. He also loved the Egyptian food that wasn't much spicy, its typical Mediterranean/Middle Eastern food. There were also several vegetarian options available at low prices. His last stop in Giza, of course, was the Great Pyramid. There were other sites to see, such as the Pharaoh's Boat. Along the ways, he stopped for buying some things from the children from Khan El Khalili Bazar. His trip wouldn't be completed with a visit to this bazar which is the oldest bazaar in Cairo. Speaking about his experience he says, "This bazaar was a loud, crowded, colorful and an exciting place, filled with all kinds of foods and shiny baubles. In this bazaar was a spice market where one can easily find fresh spices of any kind. There was also a perfume market with the countless mixing of scents of essential oils. Deeper into the market were gold vendors and antique shops that were filled with interesting pieces. There was also a fabric shop and carpet vendors and seller of almost everything you might desire." Speaking further about the history of this Bazar Tariq explained, "It dates back to 14th century when Emir Dajaharks Al-Khalili built a market on the site of Za'afran tomb that was the place of Fatimid rulers of Egypt. The most easily recognizable landmark at the verge of Khan El Khalili was the huge Al Hussain mosque, one of the most attractive sacred sites in all of Egypt. Its gothic revival architecture makes it instantly recognizable, Café owners beckon welcomingly at empty seats, inviting Tariq. The cafes in the area were in beautiful old buildings with geometric wood paneling, typical of Islamic architecture. Vendors saunter through the crowds, eager to show off their wares. Tariq experience of Khan El Khalili was unforgettable.

During his stay in Egypt, he also visited Jamat Al Azhar and met Sheikh Al Azhar also referred as Sheikh Tantavi, which was founded in 970 AD, as the heart of the newly formed Fatimid city. Sheikh Mohammed Sayed Tantawi, exercised great influence, if not actual authority, within the faith. For the West, he was an expressive proponent of moderate Islam, eager to engage in dialogue on interfaith tolerance. Al Azhar is still a leading center of Islamic theology and its grand Sheikh is the top religious cleric in Egypt, advising the state on religious matters and providing religious guidance to the country and the greater Muslim world.

It is of the first mosque in Cairo, its Sheikh is considered as the highest theological authority for the Egyptian Muslims. Tariq was very fond of the ancient architecture so he looked around the building which was the pleasant blend of different architectural styles. The chamber of the tomb, located over a doorway on the left side, just inside the entrance, was a beautiful mihrab which was to indicate the direction of Mecca. Sheikh Al Azhar is the prominent title in Egypt and considered as the highest authority in the Sunni thought. A madrassa was established here in AD 988, developing into a university which is the world's second-oldest learning institution. At one time the university was one of the world's famous centers of learning, drawing students from Europe and all over the Islamic kingdom. The large contemporary campus (due east) is still the most significant place to study Sunni theology.

Due to his love for architecture and local culture of the Muslim world, Tariq couldn't resist himself from visiting Muhammad Ali mosque in Cairo. Egypt was an endless fascination country filled with a rich earliest history and culture. It was more than Pyramids of Giza, it was also occupied with ancient archaeological reserves. Tariq's family lived in Egypt for over 4 years so they all spent a good deal of time discovering this vast country. Muhammad Ali mosque was specially made by Muhammad Ali Pasha between 1830 and 1848.

Tariq with his wife Parveen, Daughter Fouzia and Shazia, Sons Atif and Saquib
at Muhammad Ali Mosque - Cairo

This mosque was the largest of its kind to be made in the first half of 19th century. He visited the mosque along with his family. Speaking about the beauty of this mosque Tariq explained, "This mosque was built using Ottoman style architecture. It was built with a dome in the center that was surrounded by four small domes. Two stunning cylindrical Turkish minarets with balconies were set on the west wind of the mosque. The main material used was limestone with lower story and forecourt tiled with alabaster. After entering the Citadel gates, they walked uphill to the domed structured decorated with slender minarets. Inside, the domes gave a spacious feel to the prayer hall. The outside courtyard offers a commanding view, albeit a hazy

one. This famous landmark was surrounded by other building including Al-Gawhara Palace, Mosque of Suleiman Pasha, National Military Museum and Royal Carriage Museum.

Along with traveling, Tariq also loved to read religious books and novels. Before entering high school, Tariq was very fond of reading. His parents always encouraged him to read books. As he entered the college, he started reading some religious books his father always told him about. His love for books made him understand a few things. First is that for many students, the method of doing book reports and reading compulsory texts is boring and uninspiring. "I found my love of reading when I had the autonomy to decide what I read and read at my own pace without a deadline or piles of work in the way," says Tariq.

Even since Tariq was little, he loved to read and write. His desire to read religious books was very strong. It was his passion and he strongly believed that fulfilling his passion made him happy, it encouraged him to try to work harder, relieved his stress and took him to another virtual world away from the busy lives. He always loved the company of books and novel and has a mini library at home full of religious and scholarly books. He usually preferred religion, spirituality, war, history, and poetry. His passion for reading was so strong that once if he starts reading a book he can't keep it down until he finished it. Being surrounded by books always brings him satisfaction. Some might see the library as a boring location, but for me, my day will not be complete without visiting my library, says

Tariq. Reading was the most incredible and important skill Tariq learned throughout his life. For him, the library introduced a world of adventure, new ideas and different ways of thinking. Tariq passion for penetrative and extensive reading has unequivocally confirmed the truth of a statement once made by the French Philosopher, "Only passions, great passions can elevate the soul to great things." My soul, not merely my intellect, has indeed been elevated to greatness, says Tariq.

Tariq absolutely loved Shakespeare throughout his academic career with the exception of *Julius Caesar*. He was reading things he didn't fully understand at a fast pace, the pieces he read were boring, to be frank, and writing reports on it afterward were not fun in the least. He read his comedies in class as well, and the writing wasn't drastically different from what he already read, but the leisure of reading at his pace with no obligations, and forming his own opinions on the book was a new, refreshing experience. Shakespeare was captivated by the word 'world'. He used it at least 650 times in his printed writings, from poems written in his twenties to disturbing late plays such as The Winter's Tale and The Tempest.

Tariq loved Shakespeare because it gave him pleasure while reading his novels, particularly when they were about love. The depths in his novels and the intricacy behind each story was the few things he loved. The climatic sound of battles, the clash of swords, the greedy violence, the seeds of ambition, the fight for justice, the corruption of a kind, no theme was left untouched by Tariq. There will always be a respected place for him in the history of English language, because what he says is universal, appealing to our deepest thoughts and stirring our darkest secrets, says Tariq. Shakespeare's play expressed different aspects of life that transcend time. Love, revenge, war and political intrigue, are just a few themes found in his work which are applicable to any age. Tariq continued reading him enthusiastically because those themes can be still connected to one's own time.

Tariq believes that reading is a desire which makes our lives more expressive and that everybody has that desire to some degree. Though, there are a lot of difficulties from us understanding that; for me, it was compulsorily reading with limits for school and wasting 30-60 min of every day reading for my parents. Everybody has experienced this and for many, it makes it difficult to find joy through literature. I do believe, however, that given the right book and the right conditions, anyone can. But somewhere in the primary school, Tariq's love of reading faded. He also noticed how his other friends were constantly absorbed in their books. He wasn't like that. The transition from learning to read to reading to learn was uneventful for him, like the way one-day blends into the other.

Books are the one thing that can tell stories despite time and age; they let explore worlds we will never see; and they help us see our own world through the eyes of the strong, weak, privileged, marginalized, intelligent, impaired and countless other perspectives. Literature connects people, teaches lessons, entertains, and more often than not makes us better people. Sometimes, for people like me, we just need the right kind of push before we dive headfirst into the limitless waters," he clarifies. His standout favorite reason though to be passionate about reading would have to be because it gives you a great perspective on life outside of you.

After I graduated from university, I made an effort to read books for fun. I craved the knowledge and satisfaction that radiated from my friends after a good read, like a runner's high. I wanted to know what it felt like to stay up all night with a good book, to relax in a comfy chair and forget about time," says Tariq. An escape from job responsibilities and badminton practices and the opportunity to ignite the reading spark He had lost years ago was hard to resist.

Tariq visited UAE that is famous for the extravagance of elevated structures and the top of line shopping centers. Tariq and his wife took Emirates airline and reached Dubai. The temperature there was hot and it was the month of March. It was the tourist's season in Dubai so the crowd was more than expected and prices were also a bit higher.

Dubai is an avatar of wealth, quick-blooming skyscrapers, opulent hotels, and a mall with an indoor ski slope. There was no shortage of hotels in Dubai, particularly the luxury hotels.

Just like any other major city and tourist area, there was a lot of traffic in Dubai. There was also a rush hour traffic the time we were coming from the airport. I was aware of the working days in Dubai so we decided to visit Burj Khalifa on weekend. As traffic in Dubai is much lighter on the weekends, says Tariq. We used the regular taxi for the best prices and asked the driver for the price and reached the hotel. Dubai has a clean and easy to use Metro system. During the week and rush hours, this might be the best choice due to traffic issues. Though the day Tariq and his wife used Metro, it was not much crowded.

Tariq visited Dubai with his wife, as it was one of his favorite places to visit. To believe in the beauty of that city, it must be seen with one's own eyes. Dubai is considered a haven for adventures seekers. He visited one of the main attraction of Dubai and the world's tallest building, Burj Khalifa. Like thousands of people, Burj Khalifa also draws Tariq to marvel at its view. Speaking about the marvel of Burj Khalifa, Towering high in the Emirati sky in the heart of Dubai is their Burj Khalifa, the tallest structure made by humans. This building redefined the limits of human's abilities, combining with cutting-edge technology with delicate cultural influences which came together splendidly to create this icon. Tariq visited the observation decks which are at 124th, 125th and then 148th floor that was a truly humbling experience. At the other side of Burj Khalifa was Dubai Marina with Palm Jeremiah and Burj Al Arab. On the complete opposite of this site as the Dubai Airport and Old Dubai with the souks. Along this strip was Jumeirah Beach filled with beach resorts, shops, and restaurants.

Tariq further elaborated his visit to Burj Khalifa, "It will draw your breath as you stand before it and struggle to crane your head all the way back to take a look at its length. You might not be able to see its tip at sometimes as the combination of height and glaring sunshine all the way up there might blind you.

Mr. and Mrs. Tariq at Burj al Arab - UAE

Getting into Burj Khalifa was not easy and straightforward, Tariq and his wife went there through the Dubai Mall. From there he directly came out to the floor of Burj Khalifa. He bought his tickets to climb to the top and joined the long queue. As they entered they were stooped at the entrance gate where a guard verified their details, the car plate numbers and then allowed them access. As they walked through the huge, impressive lobby, marked by a unique drum-cymbal décor, they get past the doors made of glass that can be opened only the access card, and then took the lift. They went straight to the 125th and 148th floor to enjoyed the view from up there as it was the most important to do while visiting Burj Khalifa. With its towering skyscrapers, ultra-luxurious hotels and outlandish opulence, this city on the Persian Gulf fueled by tourism and oil money resemble a cross between Hong Kong and Las Vegas, says Tariq.

Tariq with his wife Parveen at iconic Burj al Arab - UAE

Further explaining the beauty of the world's tallest building Tariq says, "The Burj also is an engineering marvel and entertaining attraction. Several times a day, throngs of tourists are treated to a Bellagio-style fountain show set to Arabic, classical and international

music on a 30-acre lake at the base of the building. Indeed, both sets of fountains were designed by the same company. The Burj's fountain shoots water jets as high as 50 stories."

On his return from Burj Khalifa, he also visited Palm Jumeirah. In the city full of world-breaking wonders and awe-inspiring architecture, the man-made Palm Jumeirah stands out one of the most intriguing and enticing places for visitors and locals. Palm Jumeirah is an engineering and design feat, an oasis of entertainment and luxury on the Persian Gulf, situated on the island which resembles a palm tree. Tariq started his day at the magnificent Palm Jumeirah and it was like a success unlike any other. Palm Jumeirah is an artificial archipelago off the Jumeirah coast in Dubai. Built out of land reclaimed from the sea, Palm Jumeirah is considered to be one of the poshest locales in Dubai. A walk in the Palm Jumeirah showed Tariq the most luxurious homes, hotels, recreational centers, restaurants and beach clubs. At this modern hub of activity in Dubai, he also enjoyed the world famous Aqua venture Waterpark at Atlantis the Palm, went for a kayak tour of the islands and for a cruise around the island. The sight of the islands, branching out into the sea is a sight to behold and truly unforgettable, says Tariq. Tariq spent half of his day near poolside at Sofitel the Palm which was a wonderfully cathartic experience. Just being on the Palm Jumeirah gave him the feeling as if he is out of the city and away from the crowds.

He also enjoyed the beautiful route to Palm Jumeirah through Dubai's Sheikh Zayed Road to the island onboard the luxury and weather controlled atmosphere of the Hop-On/Hop-Off Big Bus Dubai Tour, which was one of his preferred Dubai exploration tours – one of the best methods to travel Dubai, particularly for first-timers, says Tariq. The next day he visited the Dubai museum with his wife. The museum is housed in Al Fahidi Fort that was built in 1787, the oldest building in the city. In the museum, Tariq encountered colorful dioramas and exhibits which depicted everyday life.

Tariq with his wife Parveen at historic Al Fahidi Fort Gallery

They entered the Al Fahidi fort gallery by descending down the spiral stairways located at the South Western tower of the fort. The gallery consisted of artifacts leading up to the 1960's when the oil was discovered. The artifacts on the display were both local as well as things that were collected through trade with other countries. Dubai Museum is so simple outside but inside, a treasure trove awaits.

An underground picture of fort taken by Tariq

Underground section was devoted on depicting a view of old Dubai's occupants and their way of life. As Tariq was very interested in history, he couldn't miss the opportunity to get the rich, full and integral knowledge of the old history of Dubai that interacted with different people and civilization across history. The galleries in the museum feature the historic Arabic houses, mosques, souks, date farms, desert and marine life. All features of past Dubai life, both marine, and desert-dwelling were covered in subsequent displays. There was also an exhibit showing pearl diving, with sets of peal merchants' weights, scales, and sieves. There were also artifacts from Africa and Asia and other archaeological digs which dates back to the third millennium BC.

Tariq with his wife Parveen at the fascinating Sheikh Zahid Mosque - Abu Dhabi

After visiting, Burj Khalifa, he also visited the Grand Mosque in Abu Dhabi with his wife.

Abu Dhabi was located approximately 1 to ½ hours of driving distance from Dubai depending on the traffic. He always wanted to visit one of the world's largest Mosque because of its great architectural work of art. This mosque has the capacity for around 40,000 worshipers. It features around 28 domes, over 1,000 columns and 24-carat gold gilded chandeliers and the world's largest hand-knotted carpet. The main prayer hall is dominated by one of the world's largest chandelier. The first ceremony at the mosque was the funeral of its namesake, Sheikh Zayed, who is buried at this site. During his visit to the mosque, Tariq took some truly spectacular photos. He visited the mosque after the sunset because he wanted to see the mosque lit up. The mosque bad a dressing code which is very strict because of it a religious site. One of my favored elements of the Sheikh Zayed Grand Mosque is that its design unites the world. Several artisans and materials came from all over the world: Italy, Morocco, Germany, Pakistan, Turkey, Greece, United Kingdom, and the United Arab Emirates to name just a few, says Tariq.

Speaking about the Chandelier Tariq explained, it was imported from Germany and is made from gold and several Swarovski crystals. The carpet was hand-made by thousands of Iranian craftsmen and is the largest and most expensive carpet in the world. There are also several beautiful patterns and design containing the verses of the Quran on the wall. Sheikh Zayed Mosque is not just a huge architecture, it is also an exceptionally beautiful one. Domes and minarets have always been the important parts of Islamic architectures. This Mosque has 82 domes of various sizes and 4 minarets. The plain white color of this building, the floral design of the pillars, those reflective pools around the mosque, and the traditional Moroccan artwork under the domes are some of the things that define the beauty of this mosque, says Tariq. Tariq expressed his feeling when he first entered the Mosque, "From the moment you enter this place of worship you feel like entering into a completely different world. Everything becomes utterly calm and peaceful and there's nothing but the beauty of this mosque for you to cherish.

Tariq with his wife Parveen at Sheikh Zahid Mosque - Abu Dhabi

At night the mosque's spectacular illumination reflects the cycle of the moon. One of the minarets also houses a library featuring rare calligraphy and Arabic manuscripts. For people with little interest in religion, this landmark building is worth visiting for the architecture alone. Reminiscent of the Taj Mahal with its white marble domes, the building was completed in 2008 and combines Mamluk, Ottoman and Fatimid styles.

Tariq standing in front of Willis Tower - Chicago, USA

He also visited Sears Tower in Chicago, which is now known as Willis Tower. This tower is the tallest building in the US, a 1,450-foot modern office block which offers unrivaled views of Chicago. His highly anticipated trip to Chicago turned out to be a really great day filled with memories. He did it in a different way, he took the train in for half of the journey. The closest Metra train station to Madison was in Harvard, IL so he went there. It was a 1 and a 1/2 hours away. On reaching Chicago he headed over to the Willis Tower to visit the Sky deck. This was one he had really been looking forward to visiting since he planned his trip to Chicago. The Sky deck has these Ledge's, basically a glass box that extends out the side of the building so you can see below you when you stand on it, says Tariq. He got there quite early in the morning and so managed to avoid any large crowd and it was the middle of the week which probably helped.

When you reach the 103rd floor Sky deck Chicago (the top observation deck in the United States), you'll be met with jaw-dropping panoramic views that can span up to four states and nearly 50 miles on a clear day. A highlight is A Ledge, a first-of-its-kind attraction that extends a glass balcony four feet beyond the building itself to create an unforgettable viewing experience from 1,353 feet up in the air. Time your visit at sunset to see the city transform from day to glittering night, says Tariq. It took a while but he finally made it back from the tower. He took the Metra commuter train in from Harvard, IL at 5:47 PM.

Tariq with his brother's son in law Saleem - USA

On his return, he stopped at Mister Donut and had tea. He was on a quest for donuts all the day. There were certain shapes in the American restaurant landscape that are unique, even when they've long gone out of business. Think Howard Johnson and Pizza Hut, but also the W-roof-shaped franchise Mister Donut, says Tariq. The menu was diverse and creative, with brunch until 2 p.m. and lunch and dinner after 11 p.m. Brunch has crepes, benedicts, omelets and more. He picked out a selection of the cake donuts–cherry and regular glazed.

Favorite Poet

Tariq has also studied the literature of Allama Iqbal who was a poet, philosopher, reformer and a politician born in Sialkot. Muhammad Iqbal, the poet, and philosopher, the most erudite, profound and brilliant political thinker of the Muslim world was a dominant figure in the twentieth century. He wrote his major poetic works in Urdu, Persian, and Arabic. "Iqbal wrote two books on the topic of The Development of Metaphysics in Persia and The Reconstruction of Religious Thought in Islam and many letters in the English language, besides his Urdu and Persian literary works. In which, he revealed his thoughts regarding Persian ideology and Islamic Sufism – in particular, his beliefs that Islamic Sufism activates the searching soul to a superior perception of life. He also discussed philosophy, God and the meaning of prayer, human spirit and Muslim culture, as well as other political, social and religious problems", Tariq elaborated.

Iqbal's impact on the Muslim world as one of the utmost thinkers of Islam remains unequaled. In his writings, he addressed and urged people, mainly the youth, to stand up and face life's challenges confidently. The essential theme and main source of his message were the Qur'an. In his poetry Iqbal used the metaphor of the Shaheen (falcon or eagle) mostly in reference to young Muslims, to signify the concept of constant struggle in order to contribute to the Islamic cause of serving humankind at large. He compared the tireless pursuit of this goal with the life of the scrounging vulture, who lives on animal corpses without the dignity of effort.

Appreciating Iqbal's poetic and philosophic concept, Tariq said: "He preached optimism, an active attitude towards life and man's purpose in the world, he forcefully asserted noble ideals and principles of humanism, democracy, peace, and friendship among peoples."

According to Tariq, Iqbal was an heir to a very rich literary, mystic, philosophical and religious tradition. He imbibed and assimilated all that was best in the past and present Islamic and Oriental thought and culture. His range of interests covered Religion, Philosophy, Art, Politics, and Economics, the revival of Muslim life and the universal brotherhood of man. His prose, not only in his national language but also in English, was powerful. His two books in English demonstrate his mastery of English. But poetry was his medium par excellence of expression. Everything he thought and felt, almost involuntarily shaped itself into verse. Tariq had studied Rumuz-i-Bekhudi, Zabur-i-Ajam, and the most famous of the Urdu literature work. Tariq was very fond of Iqbal's Urdu literature especially Rumuz-i.-Bekhudi because this group of poems has as its main themes the ideal community, Islamic ethical and social principles and the relationship between the individual and society. Although he is true throughout to Islam, Iqbal recognizes also the positive analogous aspects of other religions. Tariq further told about this book as, "Rumuz-i-Bekhudi is addressed to the world's Muslims. Iqbal sees the individual and his community as reflections of each other. The individual needs to be strengthened before he can be integrated into the community, whose development, in turn, depends on the preservation of the communal ego. It is through contact with others that an ego learns to accept the limitations of its own freedom and the meaning of love. Muslim communities must ensure order in life and must, therefore, preserve their communal tradition. It is in this context that Iqbal sees the vital role of women, who as mothers are directly responsible for inculcating values in their children".

Tariq found Allama Iqbal as a source of inspiration for how he presented his world beautifully and elegantly. His words flow with rhythm, his expressions come out with vitality and his views superimpose all that he has in his world. The world created by Iqbal was not an imitation in any sense of the real world we live in, but an improvement on it presented so purposely that the reader will wish to imitate that improvement. This aspect of Iqbal's poetry is also due to his perception of the beautiful in nature and art Bang-e-Dara", "Zarb-e-Kaleem is also his favorites because in this book Iqbal presented his views so strong and powerfully that the words fortify them. In addition to that, Tariq found his imaginations and views so natural that the words dotted with thoughts when jotted together seem to dance in the flow of lyrical chant. Iqbal's poetic skills are versatile. The actual spark of his poetry lies in the daintiest use of metaphor, myth, simile, metaphysical approach and unique imagery. Iqbal is adept at using different metaphors.

Taking about Shikwa and Jawab-e-Shikwa Tariq says that, "A new poem, a fresh piece, innovative thought, unique picture. This is all Iqbal's poetry is about. It is only he who has given innovative creativity and new aspects for pondering over in each of his pieces. To be remembered fondly is his most delighting creation, "Shikwa Jawab-e-Shikwa", a literary work of every time for everyone. The beautiful mixture of the interrogative and declarative pattern followed in this poem has no parallel in the history of literature. It has all in itself. Emotions, feelings, bewilderedness, piety, sinfulness, metaphors, epitome, there isn't any aspect uncovered in this magnum opus. One feels like flowing in its rhythm, moving in its tone and lost in its imagery. It is one of its kind and an example for all, for it won't get any other literary piece to beat its standards. He has awakened many dead souls by the magic of his verses in this poem, a piece which would be remembered for ages. We've hearts but dead, eyes but not wet and feelings with no warmth, this is only the power of Iqbal's words that blew some breath in the dead and mislaid nation of his time"

"Iqbal was the man, who of all the greatest poets had the most comprehensive soul. He has described everything in his lyrical words. Every aspect of life seems to be highlighted. He doesn't only describe through words but also feels them, realize the true emotions and then sketch them via words. The way he senses his words is directly passed to the reader due to their purity. Masjid-e-Qurtuba, though being a statue, is explained in such an exceptional way by him that Tariq has seen it in imagination, felt its incredibility and sensed its actuality. It is indeed standard of a great poet like Iqbal who can do such wonders. List of the miracles done by his words follows no end. He was the soul that felt things around, sensed them in true words and captured the spark of every second. He jotted every moment in letters. The dust of his creativity sparkled on pages and miracles resulted. His poetry is a perfect blend of emotions, feelings, inspiration, and enduringness. His words were the only ray of hope for the nation living in misery in his time. His views are simply actuating hopes for the youth. He won hearts, won souls, won lives. He won the word via the charm of his words. His poetry won him every nation of every time, every person of every class. No matter young or old, every single being has something for himself in his collection. His words are still the only spark of a promising future for a dangling nation like we are. He did wonders in literature. His poetry keeps no parallel. It has covered every aspect, every desire, every feeling, from ordinary to extraordinary. Indeed, Iqbal's name comes among the top in the history of literature, a person who initiated a new style of writing, a new trend of expressing and a new pattern of blowing people's lives via the fortified words," says Tariq.

The reason why Iqbal is Tariq's favorite poet s because Iqbal described vividly the pitfalls of modern Muslim and western societies, and at the same time offered immense hope to the young who were willing to embrace his vision and heed his advice. His

imagery of the dawn to come is emphatic: "See your present in the light of the past.

Tariq also used to study Iqbal's poetry in which there were so many references from the Holy Quran. Speaking of Iqbal's poetry, "There is no doubt that his poetry has universality and would continue benefitting the whole world. His poetry contains endless messages and his work in the field of literature is of supreme importance still. The most prominent feature of his work was that he always emphasized the importance of religion. Islam to him was very much important and because of this, he had an urge for a separate homeland in which Muslims could practice their religion freely. He had a great vision and he perceived future critically. He was very much aware of the sufferings of Indian Muslims and finally, he used his pen like a sword in order to pierce the darkness that was embedded in the hearts and the minds. His words were influential to such an extent that ultimately they brought a fruitful result in the form of an independent state. The themes of his poetry were of great importance and still, they are regarded as a great source of inspiration. His concept of "Self" (khudi) is based on the concept of self-realization which integrates all the known facts of the universe into a single unity, and this single unity is the concept of God. His concept of self-realization is not merely based on Divine power, rather he highlighted that in order for us to seek the truth of our existence; proper training, experiences, and education plays a vital role".

Tariq also remembered Iqbal's emphasis on education. He was very much aware of the Importance of "education", and according to him, education is the sole of a human being which creates selflessness and generosity. He focused on the youth's education because he knew that youth would hold the future, and without the intellect and proper education future would all be murky and gloomy for Muslims. Tariq has a firm belief that Iqbal's vision and voice, which changed the destiny of Indian Muslims, is what is needed today to liberate Pakistanis from the chains that bind their bodies, hearts, minds, and souls.

Favorite Subjects

Favorite subjects are the one which a person can enjoy without getting bored. Every person has their own interest and it varies from person to person. When in college and school, Tariq's favorite subject was Islamic studies and General Knowledge. At a very young age, he realized that he needed to study about Islam in a more organized manner, educate himself more on the fundamentals of Islam. He always loved studying Islamic studies as it lays the foundations of the Islamic belief system for a young child in an age-appropriate way. Tariq learned the key concepts of Tawheed, which were explained in simple language from the Quran and the teaching of Prophet Muhammad (Peace Be Upon Him). Without the doubt of given political turmoil globally and ever-present fears of terrorism and extremism, understanding Islam and the role of Muslims in the contemporary world is increasingly vital. The students of today, if properly taught, will become the teachers of the future with a vision for multiculturalism and peaceful co-existence, says Tariq. Tariq during his early age discovered that Islamic knowledge is beautiful and exciting to learn and that his life would begin to revolve around it. Speaking about Islamic studies Tariq explained that, "I have learned so much from the Seerah and Stories of Prophets which are a great way to teach young Muslims the valuable lesion and provide them with the role models. But sadly most of the institutes teach these stories as historical facts without delving into any significant lessons".

Most of the Islamic studies teachers whom Tariq have met in his college and school were so motivated to make a difference. Such teachers have an inspiring impact on their students. It is only those who teach Islam with passion, love, enthusiasm and the desire to ignite change that can motivate students and get them to love Islam and want to practice it.

The other subject which Tariq liked the most was General Knowledge. He used to study general knowledge for hours without getting bored. Tariq was introduced to general knowledge when he was in Grade 1. As he grew up and went to higher classes, he did not only study general knowledge books prescribed by the school but also borrowed such books from the library to expand his knowledge. Looking at his interest in the subject Tariq's father brought him so many magazines about general knowledge which are still with him in his personal library. He eagerly waited for it every month and finished reading the entire magazine in around three days. He read them over and over again to memorize the facts. Through learning general knowledge, he also earned appreciated in this subject at his school, home as well as in his friend's circle. This inspired him to read and learn all the more. His teachers always recommended his name for any GK quiz competitions. He has taken parts in so many competition and has won prizes for his school. Anyone was able to judge Tariq's personality by his up-to-date general knowledge of various subjects and current affairs.

General knowledge helped Tariq grow both on personal as well as academic level. It narrowed his sense of perceiving the world, understanding and analyzed the situation better as one would without proper knowledge. It opened the gateways of thinking for Tariq and took it to the level from where the whole world seemed to be a better place. This world is unpredictable and we all need to stay aware and vigilant. Having general knowledge is the sign of an educated and intelligent being. It helps to grow your confidence level. You can start a conversation with anybody on any ongoing topic and your knowledge would impress the person you are interacting with, says Tariq. Tariq did not attain general knowledge overnight. He was in constant touch with the entire world in order to gain as much knowledge as possible. Reading newspapers and listening to the news channels was the important practice he adopted for staying updated. Another interesting medium he used to gain knowledge was through quizzes. Tariq was able to ease himself into any conversation because he was armed with general knowledge. It allowed him to talk his way into the interesting conversation with practically anyone. He thrived in most of the social setting because he was able to talk about anything. He had a good grasp of current events which a great conversation starter. He was also aware of other culture and facts about other countries which helped in thrive in multicultural interaction. It is knowledge which has equipped man with the limitless power with which man dominates over all beings who are physically much stronger than him. Knowledge has significantly helped him to conquer the nature and this conquest has prompted human progress and civilization, says Tariq.

One of the advantages which Tariq gained from learning general knowledge was that it broadens his mind to possibilities and allowed him to experience with the world for what it's worth. Knowing what's happening to the world around us through current events, appreciating how we got to where we are today through history, and understanding the many other persons, places, cultures, and scientific discoveries allowed Tariq to immerse in experiences far beyond the walls of the classroom. Tariq never gets tired of continuing the quest for greater knowledge. His thirst for knowledge was never satisfied. Speaking about the importance of general knowledge Tariq says, "Every human being has a drive for knowledge. Knowledge brings power to life. Those who have awareness are capable of commanding others and ruling the world. But the power that comes from knowledge should be used for the growth of mankind and not be misused. I truly realize that humanity comes with knowledge even as power flows from it. Knowledge plays an important role in life. Unluckily in today's world of strife and endless warfare, the power that is imposed at gunpoint is an obligation and not an asset".

Sports Career

Tariq started his badminton career in 1956. He participated in National Championship that was conducted in Lahore and Karachi. "The "spirit" of Badminton includes a proper attitude concerning the game – a perspective that considers, for one, that there are no opponents – only participants. Aspirants, if you prefer, demanding the best of themselves… working, perhaps, in a sort of conflicting harmony – the barometer of excellence being determined by doing the best we can… extending ourselves to pursue the limits of our abilities and endurance. The ultimate in ourselves being shown on the court and off the court as well," says Tariq.

He often secured first and second positions in the matches. When he was in grade six, he traveled through the train that delivered goods because of no funds from school and Sindhi Badminton Administration. During his college days, he always took part in badminton tournaments. For inter-university Championship, the selection for potential players was conducted in Shikarpur or Larkana. After getting selected from here, the next step was to play with Sindhi University's best players. Those who showed great energy and passion and stood first got selected. Tariq always reserved first positions in the selection trials. During the matches, he used all the things to the best of his advantage and always stayed calm and composed. Tariq was focused on just one task of winning the title, in which he remained successful. He played clever shots when it mattered the most and took the first game 21-15 in 23 minutes,

His favorite aspect of playing badminton is that he was able to play it during school breaks and at home after class in their free time. Also, badminton is a simple sport for children who need to relax after class and it is an easygoing sport which doesn't need much physical strength. At that time, I was in grade three. My primary school, that was just a few minutes' walks from my home, had a nice badminton court." says Tariq. My parents are very fond of sports, particularly badminton and football. My father even used his own money to purchase some plastic balls for children in my village to play for free. Every evening, my father taught me and some friends of mine to play badminton at the school's badminton court. Those were happy times. I've been very interested in badminton since then," he revealed.

The most common fears a personal experience, which often sabotage all hope for success, are the fears of failure, poverty, and loss of money. These fears cause people to avoid the risk of any kind and to reject opportunity when it is presented to them. They are so afraid of failure that they are almost paralyzed when it comes to taking any chances at all. But Tariq was never afraid of anything in his life. He was filled was passion and desire to accomplish his goals. "The most common reaction in a fear situation is the attitude of, "I can't!" This is the fear of failure and loss that stops people from taking action. It is experienced physically, starting in the solar plexus. When people are really afraid, their mouth and throat go dry, their heart starts

pounding. Sometimes they breathe shallowly and their stomach churns. Often they feel like getting up and running to the bathroom, says Tariq". The reason why Tariq never feared anything in life was that he always encouraged his curious nature. It's very clear that when you become curious about different things in life, you get little chance to think about your fear. It does not mean that you are avoiding your fear, but it helps to focus your mind productively. The purpose of doing this is to change your way of thinking or perceiving. The things you are scared of may not be actually that much fearful as you think. Even curious nature will help you to know more and more about your fear.

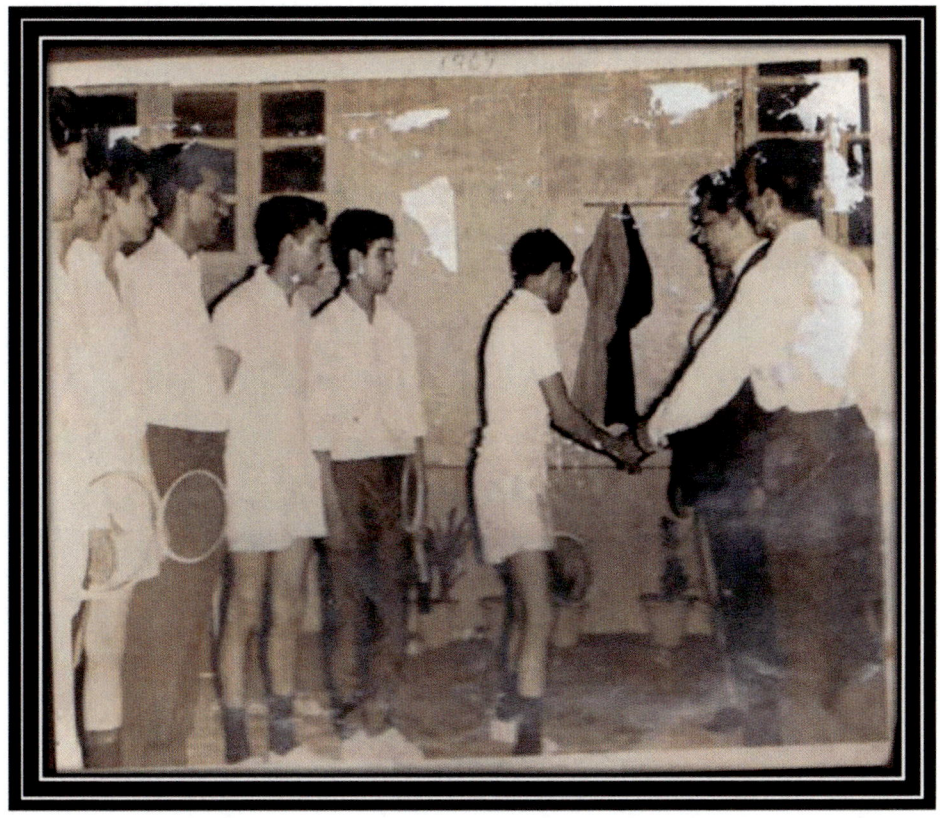

Tariq and fellow players meeting Commissioner Income Tax, Karachi Division in All Pakistan Open Championship Tournament in 1969

Fear is just an emotional reaction in response to a perceived threat, you have to drive the thoughts in the right direction to get rid of this emotional factor. If you think positively, you will find thousands of ways to win over your distressing thoughts. Try to fill your mind with positivity through hypnosis, yoga, or meditation. A positive mind will help to think more about the success factors, rather than only projecting the possible dangers, says Tariq.

He often played badminton at his primary school and received the prize in district level badminton championships from grade four to eight. "I like this sport because it is a simple way of staying healthy and making more associates. This sport is easy to play and doesn't cost much for us as we are poor students in a rural area," Tariq says. According to Tariq, the educational system of Pakistan after partition was not good enough and there were very fewer opportunities because of low budgets. He faced many hardships during his educational career, the burden of educational fees was one of the most critical ones. As he belongs to a poor rural family his father struggled hard and managed to bear his educational expenses. The rural parts of Sindh where Tariq was living at that time were in the state of abject poverty. Tariq also faced some problems in his sports career. No matter how successful, talented or lucky a sportsman appears to be, he will never experience a smooth sailing throughout their career. As a successful athlete, Tariq developed specific capacities to handle all the challenges and create benefits for himself out of it. He struggled through his sports career with resilience, optimism, and confidence. He had a strong internal drive and were open to new experiences. While some players might naturally have more of these traits than others, it can be developed through relevant support and coaching. Friends and family were the only vital source of support for Tariq. He could never have survived without the support of his family and friends.

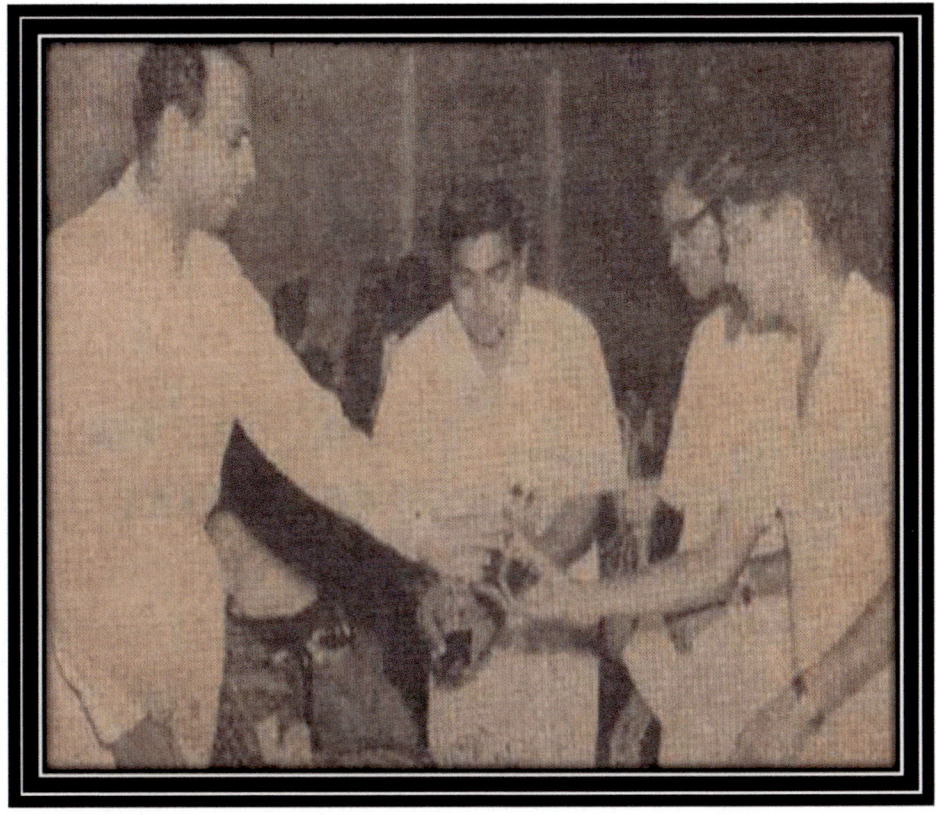

Tariq receiving the trophy from Deputy Commissioner Sukkur, Rohri

According to Tariq, "In Badminton, the golden rule is completely applicable – your conduct and your appreciation of the spirit of Badminton will most generally reflect the treatment and consideration other players will give you. Give others the respect you would like for yourself… the results will be amazing. The advantage of playing badminton is that you get a chance to socialize with people. Playing sports is quite challenging but it's good for health and improves the overall being. My life would have incomplete without sports. It was my hobby and my passion at the same time. It's something which I was used to and most enjoyed doing. I love the challenges and participation in the tournaments. It built my confidence and my ability to make quick decisions at the right time.

In a country where cricket takes precedence over other sports, one often hears athletes and other sports persons lamenting about the lack of funding. Same was the case with Tariq he traveled to Karachi for playing his first Badminton Championship, he had no shoes and badminton kit because there was no attention paid by the authorities. He borrowed all these things from a close friend and participated in the championship and won the award of National Badminton Champion. He remained National Badminton Champion for 6 years. Another incident of the same nature happened when he was traveling from Rohri to Karachi for National Badminton Championship, he had no financial support and sponsorship from the authorities and he had no money to buy shoes, badminton kit and even for the ticket. It was a financial turmoil all over again. It was so tough and frustrating as Tariq felt he had put in all this hard work for so many years to come to this point and he hadn't really got many rewards for it."

Seeing his situation, his school headmaster Badar-ud-din, who had a Sindhi background and was a good Urdu speaker provided him the badminton kit and shoes. He also asked his Hindu friend Sham Lal who was the guard of the train that carried goods, who allowed Tariq to travel on that train. After a four days long journey Tariq reached Karachi and participated in National Badminton Championship.

Tariq also played indoor games tournament organized by PIACEU Sports Club that was set up in Karachi. The tournament was held at Airport club and EDH for the staff of Airline. This club was formally inaugurated by the Industrial Relations Managers who also gave some sports goods from the PIA Welfare Fund. The corporation also gave assurance for necessary support regarding club premises and materials etc. Along with badminton, other games were also played which included table-tennis, chess, and carom. The matches lasted for four weeks after which the club conducted football, hockey, volleyball and cricket matches. At the inauguration ceremony of the club, the PIACEU Secretary-General Qazi Ahsan Shamim said it was for the first time that the staff would have the regular facility for playing games and sports. In the image below are the position holders of PIACEU club.

Tariq Khan (Joint Secretary Indoor Games) Khalil -Ur-Rehman (Secretary PIACEU Club), Mr, Riaz Ali (Joint Secretary Outdoor Games)

Tariq (Joint Secretary indoor games) participated in PIACEU Sports Club (Jan 01, 1976)

While playing badminton competitively, Tariq also started coaching the young juniors. He had all the important elements that a badminton player must have in order to make it big in the badminton world. Tariq's talent was God-given whereas he acquired the physical ability through training and exercises. Badminton was not a cheap game at that time, and above all the memberships and lessons all cost money. Tariq was unable to pay for all those fees, and it seemed impossible to win a national title. But he was financially supported by his family. The path to becoming a successful player got smaller and smaller just like a bull's eye. From school and college to the National Championship, it becomes a tiny dot. Very few people in the world can achieve it. Without financial support from the family,

it would be extremely hard for Tariq to achieve the ultimate goal. The hardest thing Tariq faced while he was a child, the willingness to work and the desire to win, the passion to become a champion. Some of the people call is the fighting spirit but Tariq calls it the intensity and desire to win. That was the one skill Tariq found very difficult to learn. There can't be any excuses. The next day after training and game, even if he wakes up and feel tired, he had to overcome the fatigue, pain and the other excuses to continue working.

Looking back, Tariq says her mother was totally involved with him in the game. During those growing up years, she made him eat a lot, made him stronger that he could compete in the tournament and pushed him a lot. Tariq's phenomenal motivation and dedication to stay focused on badminton don't come as a surprise to those who have known about his dream of being a national level badminton champion. He liked to excel whether it was in the warm-up sprints or the off-court physical training. The way he would react to the rigorous training was commendable. Those were the days when Tariq used to carry two bags. One contained his badminton kit and the other his college books. Badminton is not a prominent sport like cricket, where you have more probabilities of making it. But Tariq had the confidence in himself that he would make it, that he would get the results and therefore he chose badminton. He became the captain of badminton team in 1964. This title, along with his selection in the inter-university Hyderabad team, signaled to everyone that he was indeed Pakistan's rising badminton star. While he was scorching the courts, he continued to study and never compromised on his grades. He managed the time well between badminton and school. It was one of the greatest challenge for Tariq to manage his time equally for studies and badminton, but as he was clear on his goals, he carried education and sport together. He was devoting equal time to his studies in school and college. Every sportsman has the invariable task to study and compete, for Tariq, it was like having two daytime jobs. The balance was crucial for him because of competitive sports and academic work side by side in the life of a sportsman. He always knew when his exams and midterms will be and when the badminton competitions. He had the habit of managing his academic calendar and the timetable for exams in advance. Students often find it hard to strike a balance between sports and academics. But maintaining this balance is not impossible; there are many famous sportsmen who have achieved success on both these fronts, says Tariq. His parents always motivated him to effectively manage his time between sports and studies. Tariq has seen most of his fellows who find it difficult to keep pace with academics. Most of them missed half of their classes and prepare for the exam at the eleventh hour. The reason why Tariq was able to find the balance between studies and sports was the undeniable support of his parents. His parents played many roles, that of a motivator, a caretaker, and a helper. He would not be able to cope up with his studies if he failed to get the guidance of teachers, parents, and peers. His father Abdul Hammed Khan set the ideals for him by leading an organized life.

The attitude, behavior, and action of Tariq's parents influenced his mindset and snow the seeds of learning. His father gave him all the help and encouragement he needed to strike that desired balance.

 The key to Tariq's success was simple. Know and set your objective. Stick to a single goal – if you pursue two rabbits, both will escape. Knowing the objective clearly is vital. People with an aim in life always prosper because they know the direction they are heading towards.

Badminton Captain Badge (1963-1964)

Badminton Captain Badge (1964-1965)

In every tournament, his greatest threat was maintaining self-confidence while competing with strong opponents, and overcoming setbacks," he reflects. "Our teams have great spirit and team chants. I'm always satisfied with our performance no matter if we win or lose. We're all fully committed to the sport, despite most of us being new to it".

During the 70's, Pakistani badminton players were known for their stroke play and modish wrist work. Conventional coaching in Pakistan also highlighted making a point rather than overwhelming your opponents. Though, to counter the enormous speed, strength and strengths of top national players, Tariq developed his own violent and active playing style and training regime. He tried with different training practices as well as consideration and imagining techniques with progressively better results. He also embarked on a grueling and physically active training routine, finally leading to the top positions. The results that Tariq had achieved in all his career have been unbelievable and really show that hard work pays off. It is this ability to live and lead life by such righteous ideas that have delivered Tariq with the moral extent to push and yet motivate youngsters to achieve their potential. All of his achievement speaks for themselves.

Tariq with his cousin brother Khaliq with Commission Khairpur when he won
Open All Pakistan Championship Tournament

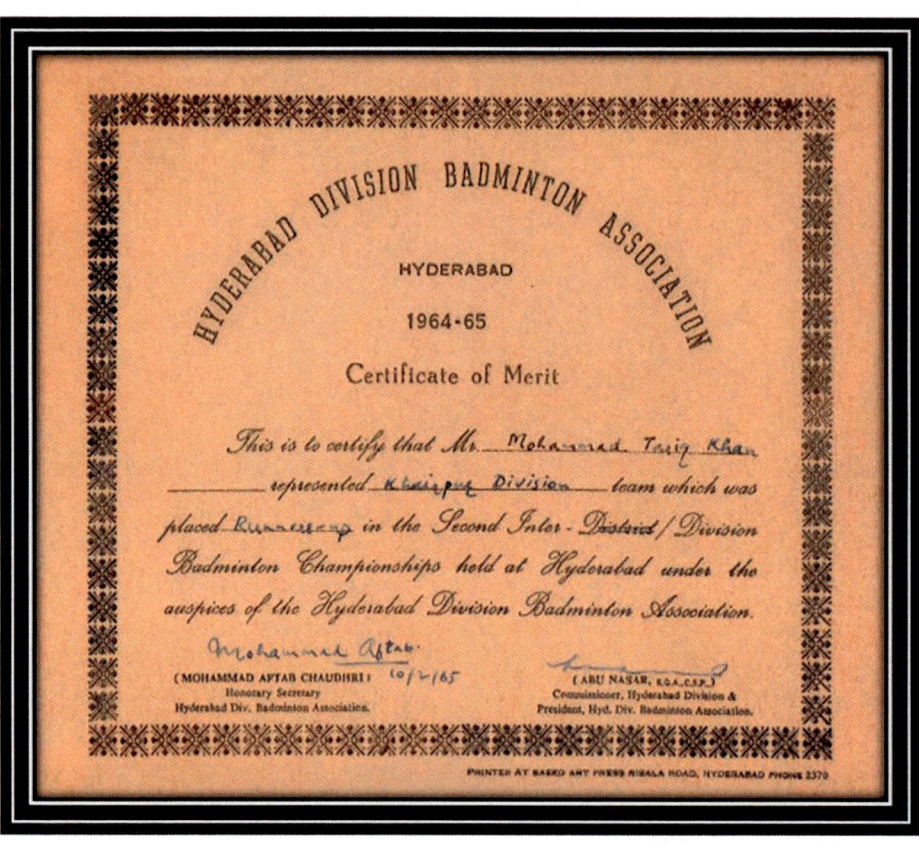

Tariq's Certificate of Merit for playing Badminton Championship held at Hyderabad

Achievements

Tariq's achievements started from his participation in matches at the college level to lead the KDBA team for nationals. He presented the University of Sindh in Inter-Varsity Badminton Championship that was held in Karachi. He was the captain of the team at that time. It was the 12th National Badminton Championship in which he was leading the Khairpur Division Team. He was leading the team because he had all the fitness, power, agility and skills needed in badminton players. He was an expert in different strokes like smash, toss, drop on the forehand, around and blackhead. Badminton is an extremely fast-paced game and it requires excellent reflexes. Tariq possessed all the speed and deception that make it harder to anticipate shots. His ability to reacting quickly towards finesses and power shot allowed him to make his way at the top positions. After leading his team in KDBA he later joined the Hyderabad team for inter-university matches. According to Tariq, badminton is not all about physical strength, it also requires a good strategy to make the correct shot at the right time either it's a drop shot, smash or clear. He was the best in identifying the weakest point of his opponents, especially in doubles. His strategy was simple, he knew that his opponents who are weak at backhand, then it is vital to hit the shuttle towards their backhand more.

Mohammad Tariq, Captain, Khairpur Division Badminton team.

Tariq to lead KDBA team for nationls

ROHRI, April 10:—Mohammad Tariq Khan of Rohri Cement Works will lead the Khairpur Division Badminton team which leaves today for Karachi to participate in the twelth National Badminton Championship.

The team comprises:
Mohammad Tariq Khan (Captain), Ghulam Ahmed and Khaliq-ur Rehman (Khairpur); Abdul Majeed, Iftikhar Ahmed, Mahmood and Badar Zaman (Sukkur) and Shakir Abdullah (Jacobabad).

Tariq to lead KDBA team for Nationals

He has also played KPT tournament on 15th Sep 1969 and then qualified for BFA.

BFA semi-final of Inter-Club that was played on 7th Oct 1969. They qualified for this semi-final when they defeated PIA by three games to one at the KPT Hall. Naseeruddin of the PIA team failed to turn up for the match and thus PIA went is arrears by two games in which the BFA obtained walk-overs.

Badminton players who participated in KPT tournament (From left to right) Abu-ul-Hassan Zaidi, A, H, Nagi, Akhtar Ali (Captain), Nasir-ud-din and Tariq Khan

Group Photo of K.P.T and National Gymkhana Finalists for Silver Cup Trophy
with Chief Guest Commodore Anwar Saeed, T.Pk, P.N.

This is a group photo of K.P.T and National Gymkhana finalists for the silver cup trophy. The trophy was presented by the Chief Guest Commodore Anwar Saeed Pakistan Navy.

In the remaining three matches BFA won its first single easily in which Azizul Qadar defeated A.H, Zaidi of the PIA team in straight two sets at 15-1, 15-2. The other single player was an interesting affair in which Saleem Farooqi from the BFA team had to struggle hard against Tariq of PIA. In both the sets, Tariq leads the score but Saleem succeeded in snatching both the sets at 15-12, 15-13. In this match, the fellow player played very well and showed a great retrieving ability. PIA, however, won its only doubles match in which Tariq Khan and A.H. Naqi played confidently against the unpredictable Fayyaz and worried Azizul Qadar. BFA was not able to settle down in this match and lost the match in the end with 2-15, 19-15. To go one level higher, to make the right choice in every hit was important, but equally essential was the ability to make the right choice for a sequence of return and to lay out a game plan for the period of a few points or even the entire match. This was the strategy Tariq played in the game.

Mr. Ansari with the Badminton Champions (Rohri)

Mr. Ansari with Badminton Champions - Rohri

He was also the part of the Hyderabadi team for inter-university badminton in which he presented Sindh University and stood 2nd. It was a Friday morning. Young shuttlers clad in their jerseys, thumping their feet against the concrete flooring welcomed everyone into their world as their coach amplifies the tone of his instructions. While talking about his humble beginnings, Tariq says:

"At a young age, parents are a huge influence. My mother has always been supportive; luckily my entire family has stood beside me through thick and thin. Life becomes so much easy when you have a supportive family. I owe my journey to them".

He also backs evolution for every player and says World badminton changes, opponents change, conditions change and the formats change, and it is important that we keep abreast. It is important that we evolve ahead of the competition. Every person with a dream of achieving something in life has to go through a difficult path of life. If you manage to overcome the hurdles and difficulties then there is nothing that can stop you from doing what you have a passion for. Same was the case with the badminton Champion Tariq. He tried but failed to achieve the name until the teenage. But he didn't lose hope at all, instead, he worked hard and achieve everything he could. His story now inspires millions of aspirants to do something great in life. The Badminton Tournaments were to start from Dec, 3rd 1975 and Tariq was excited and enthusiastic about the tournaments. There were almost 200 entries for singles and doubles. Players of all skill and grade levels were encouraged to take part in this tournament. The tournament was very interesting from the very start and every player tried his best to retain the top position. In the final of singles, Nasir-ud-din and Muhammad Tariq Khan were the opponents. In this game Nasir ud din played the confidently, applied the right strategy and won against Tariq. Whereas in doubles Tariq and Abu-Hassan Zaidi played aggressively against Nasir-ud-din and Gul Raiz and won the first match. But the second match was won by their opponents while in the third game both teams presented their best and received praise from the fans. Tariq's achievements, his focus on winning for Pakistan and his simplicity have endeared him to millions of sports fans not on a district level but nationally.

Under the supervision of Pakistan Railway, All Pakistan Badminton Championship was held in Karachi. In this championship, Tariq played final with Basit, who was a tall and strong player with a lot of achievements throughout his career. As the match started, he took Tariq and match very easy. He was overconfident in his abilities to win this match. After losing some sets from Tariq, Basit knew who he was playing with. Tariq remained the All Pakistan Champion for continuous 12 years.

He started the game with full strength and power, but after an interesting match, he lost. Tariq was again praised by his fans and took him on their shoulders. At that time the Deputy Commissioner Nusrat Hussain was the chief guest and he was impressed with the game and personality of Tariq. He invited Tariq for a cup of tea and a little talk in his office. After two days Tariq along with his father went to the office of Deputy Commissioner. During their talk, the commissioner was continuously praising Tariq and how he played during the championship. He was inspired to the level that he asked Tariq's father that he wished to make him his own son and will be responsible for all his expenses and other life necessities. Tariq's father was a man of honor, despite facing financial difficulties, he didn't agree to this and told the commissioner that he is able to bear the burden of his children and was keen on providing Tariq the education he needed.

After this incident, there was another Badminton Champion in which again Tariq scored the highest and won the final match. Till then, Nusrat Hussain promoted to the post of Commissioner Multan. He again praised Tariq on winning the game with such a great margin. He was very fond of Tariq's personalities and his attitude towards his game. Whenever Tariq scored or played an amazing shot, he couldn't help himself from congratulating him. Next day he invited Tariq to his home, He sent a protocol to the hotel where Tariq was staying who brought him to the Commissioner's home. They both shared their life experiences and future plans over a cup of tea.

One day Pakistan's renowned cricketer Shafqat Rana came to Tariq's office, Abul Hasan Zaidi introduced Shafqat Rana to Tariq and said that he has been the national champion of Pakistan, but Shafqat Rana said, "I do not agree" and challenged a match, Zaidi said, you have to play first with me". But he said he wants to play with Tariq and then played the match in which Tariq won. Tariq's Badminton career started from 1956 and ended in 1996. Over the course of 40 years, he has received numerous awards and certificates for his achievements. He served PIA for over 36 years and proved himself in every walk of life. Everyone in his surroundings was fond of his personality and his utmost passion and desire for badminton. He knew what it takes to be a professional leader every single day and what he needed to do to be at his best. This hasn't been an easy journey for him but he felt it is the right one. Having the opportunity to finish his badminton career while representing his country way the best way to end this chapter. He is also very grateful to PIA for giving him the opportunity to live his dreams and be a professional badminton player for over 40 years. Without their support, his journey wouldn't have been possible. He remembered his Badminton Championship in Karachi like it was yesterday. The feeling of representing his team was truly unlike anything else. The memories he created in this time period were something he will look back on for the rest of his life. Of course he was there to do his best in the competition, but also make sure to enjoy the entire championship experience. Get out to cheer the rest of the team members, take the time to make new associates and soak in the magical moments of the opening and closing ceremony. Those are the memories he truly cherished. He enjoyed playing badminton a lot especially with the classmates. When he played badminton, all of his worries about the homework and other things would be forgotten. He also realized that when running, he would have no stamina at all like after running less

than 500m he would get tired already, but when it comes to playing badminton, he can play for four hours or longer without resting. Champions are born as a result of several years of determination, passion, and a strong will to succeed combined with profound self-belief. Champions aren't made in gyms. They are made from something they have deep inside them: a desire, a dream and a vision. Tariq had all the skills and the will required to be a champion. He inherited the belief to succeed and he was also willing to work hard and get to the next level. He had an immense self-belief that arises out of a sheer hard work which goes into his practice sessions. The reason for his success as the support of his family, coaches and trainers that played a vital role especially in his young age. Even though when he was at the pinnacle of peak performance, he believed that his abilities can take him to greater heights. He personally felt that this quality allowed him to constantly keep raising his personal standards, He was fearless about the unknown because fear is an emotion that hampers performance and limit the natural ability of an athlete. He was never scared about his next match, he focused on what he needed to execute and go about performing his routine. He was extremely fortunate to meet and interacted with some the best badminton champions, Also, having a father who allowed his to imbibe some of this characteristics and implement those in his daily routine, made him what he is now.

Speaking about his badminton techniques he explained, "A fast sport where shuttlecock trajectory requires footwork to adjust permanently, badminton calls for extremely quick reactions in terms of both movements and court coverage in order to play the right shot. Badminton, therefore, develops coordination and also your physical flexibility. Applied to tennis, these two criteria enable you to adjust much more precisely and increase the tempo of your shots thanks to added flexibility in the upper body". He was an expert in a drop shot and anticipation and footwork. Since badminton is considered the fastest racket sports, so it is important to have a good footwork. Tariq's solid footwork would easily take the other player towards any direction on the court. Another feature that Tariq inhabited was good anticipation, the ability to sense what is happening is a matter of seconds before the other player can react. By reacting early, he has always gained a decisive advantage. He developed the skills of anticipation when he mastered the skills to play this game. By developing these skills, he was able to be at the right place at the right time, quickly analyzing the game situation and react faster.

Playing sports also require discipline, assertiveness and the ability to work as a team and the willingness to compete without fear of failure. Tariq possessed all these positive characteristics that helped him at his workplace as well as in his interpersonal relationships. Playing badminton brought out the leader inside him. He learned to handle pressure and performed under any given circumstances. Sports made him dig deep into the innermost reserves of his resources to pull out the extraordinary performances when needed. It also facilitated his inward journey of self-discovery. Playing this sport also allowed him to perform better while working for PIA where he was required to work with a group of people. Along with this he also acquired self-esteem and confidence in himself. He learned to take success and failure in the right spirit. Commenting on the kind of pressure he had to face, to win the championship, the badminton champion Tariq Kahn said in an interview, "People expect me to win. They want me to do well and finally on the court, I am playing. So I want to play for myself first and then think of the other." His attitude showed that he has trained himself to be strong and only focus on the game. Playing this sport also helped him to manage his time efficiently. He started valuing the importance of time more in his life. Sports helped him prepare, schedule and prioritize his deadline well and this built his time management skills. Tariq's impressive run in the sport has not only earned him fans but also the respect of sports-persons from various other disciplines. He surpassed the achievements of all his fellow sports-man and yet he remained down to earth and his sole focus was on the game. Anyone who knows him would know his approach towards the game. She was very headstrong and often did exert pressure on him in order to succeed. At times it does prove detrimental to him, but then the ability and skills to counter the pressure made him so much successful life. It is very important to know yourself and your opponent before any match, planning becomes easy. Understanding your strength, weaknesses and your opponent's strengths and weaknesses well and then plan the strategies accordingly. Tariq had to be prepared for the national badminton championship for a long time. He had to stay in the match and it was important to keep attacking. He fought hard, his opponent was leading in the second game (15-13), but once Tariq got the opportunity, he closed it out.

Tariq has always been a disciplined sportsperson. He was always 15 minutes earlier in practice sessions. He was much focused and could not stay away from the court for a single day. There are no cuts to success, Practice, practice till you succeed. He trained for eight hours a day, for almost 5 years. And that was not enough, one day he trained for straight 14 hours. He concentrated more on his physical fitness because badminton was more about running. He sprints, jump and hops for 65 minutes or more. Badminton is such an intense game where every point is so hard fought for, he needed enough rest between the tournaments. But he could stay a day without badminton, he only relaxed when if he had trained. "Badminton, like other sports, is an emotional marathon which requires both mental strength and endurance. It can seem like you're in the lead, but relaxing can cost you the game. It's especially hard to hold in there and make a comeback if you think you're going to lose," says Tariq.

Tariq first knew about badminton when he was a little kid. However, at that time he did not play it on a regular basis, partly because he was not fully aware of the critical importance of the physical exercises, but also because he was unable to find friends to play with. He started playing badminton when he couldn't hold the racket correctly. He used to shout and scream and yank the racket at the strong concrete-cement floor for how he couldn't hold the racket, and everyone else played the game joyfully. For him, badminton was a good way to help him pursue a healthy lifestyle. It was also an affordable type of sport as he did not have to buy a lot of specialized sports materials.

After independence over the last fifty years, the nations of India and Pakistan have clashed on both political and military fronts because of the current occupation of both nations within the states of Jammu and Kashmir. The conflict stems from both the economic welfare of the nations and from the religious differences of the people within the Indian sub-continent. The long-term religious conflicts between the Hindus and Muslim people of the region have forced the countries into countless skirmishes and three brutal wars. Due to these wars both the countries closed their doors to each other. After this China started to build his relations with Pakistan. Both the countries have been able to develop a multidimensional relationship and a good example of peaceful living. Historically, both these national shared a common threat to their security which caused to create the strong bond of entente. The past year witnessed several episodes that seriously damaged China-India relations and put them on a downward trajectory

Pakistan and China came closer after undergoing fifty years' of variations; internally and externally before arriving in the twenty-first century. For nurturing these relationships Chine sent his Sports delegation to Pakistan. This delegation was comprised of China's

Badminton Team that was comprised of their best players. Pakistan hosted the Chinese Badminton Team for a series of 5 matches. During these matched Tariq was being selected to present Pakistan and he got the opportunity to play several matches. The delegation also called for the exchanges of industrial units both in China and Pakistan, saying that investors from both sides should invest in another country to enhance their fruits of mutual investments from both the countries. 2001 marked the 50th anniversary of the establishment of Sino-Pakistani diplomatic relations and colorful celebrations were held in the two countries. In May the same year, Premier Zhu Rongji was invited to visit Pakistan. In December, President Musharraf paid a state visit to China. In January 2002, he made a stopover in Beijing on his way to Nepal to attend the SAARC Summit. In March the same year, Vice-Premier Wu Bangguo visited Pakistan as head of a Chinese Government delegation and attended the groundbreaking ceremony of Gwadar Port, a joint project to be built by China and Pakistan. Being always friendly to each other, China and Pakistan have kept close contacts in the cultural field. Since the establishment of Sino-Pakistani diplomatic relations, the two countries have sent cultural delegations and groups and held exhibitions in the other.

Tariq had been honored to present his country in badminton matches. The manager of the Chinese Badminton Team and the players didn't know much of the Urdu language but they tried to communicate in Urdu. Both the countries raised the slogan of long live friendship between China and Pakistan. Welcoming the delegation, Ambassador highlighted the deep-rooted friendship of Pakistan and China. Ambassador informed that around 22,000 Pakistani students are currently studying in China while Urdu is being taught in nine Chinese Universities as well.

According to Ambassador, the secret of China's success, being a second largest economy of the world, has been due to the hard work and commitment of the Chinese people and the good planning of the Chinese government. The Chinese players also visited the most attractive place in Pakistan. They were greeted and welcomed by the people of Pakistan. China still continues to dominate the sport but its dominance has declined because the sport is gaining popularity in other countries and they now have access to better facilities, coaches, and training techniques. Chinese players were very strong, physically fit and punctual. This is because of their well-integrated and spread out talent sourcing and grooming methods. Each and every small locality in China has its own badminton talent pool, from which the more gifted ascend through the ranks supported by the state, proving their mettle in China's national games, thereby earning the honor to represent their country and bringing glory to it and to themselves.

"One reason for the continuing superiority of Chinese badminton is the consistency in training their potential winners and champions. Intensive indoor training is imparted to players, concentrating on their weaknesses, both physical and mental. They aspire to make the player strong and fit, to successfully combat the nuances of international badminton at the highest level. Another reason was the availability and induction of former legends actively into the coaching and other talent developing areas of badminton. The young players have the opportunity to fine-tune their skills from the very people they revered on the court during their playing days and this pep up their thirst for success. They try to emulate their illustrative coaches and other training personnel, giving their best tournament after tournament. Similarly, well-equipped training centers are spread out even in the smallest localities in China. The promising talents are quickly identified and inducted into the system at a very early age, thereby providing them world-class training right from their budding years, maximizing their success later," Tariq explained.

Speaking about the friendship of Pakistan and China. Tariq expressed his views, "Pak-China undoubtedly has stood the test of time. Since 1963, when both the countries signed the border demarcation agreement, the friendship among these countries has steadily grown in strength. The authorities and people on both sides are completely aware of the significance of Pak-China relationship and are firm to strengthen it further. Both the countries are constantly moving on an ascending trajectory and gaining strength with the passage of time. Development of this astonishing relationship owes its beginning to the vision of the leadership of the two nations, who based the relationship on the values of peaceful co-existence, the unity of interests, and shared insights on regional and global progress.

Finally, CPEC has sent a message loud and clear to the regional countries and the major world powers of the determination of Pakistan and China to strengthen further their strategic partnership. India, which has upheld an aggressive attitude towards Pakistan since 1947, would not stop from using covert means to destabilize CPEC and provoke political instability in the country. China's flagship project in Pakistan is the China-Pakistan Economic Corridor (CPEC), a $46bn plan for a transport and energy corridor between China and Pakistan. CPEC will have a number of ramifications for the two counties as well as the region. CPEC could lead to political infighting in Pakistan as to who will supervise and implement projects under CPEC. "The heart of CPEC is Gwadar, which is situated in Baluchistan. It looks set to boom on the strength of Chinese investment. "There is considerable potential in Baluchistan that needs to be unearthed and harnessed," says Tariq.

Pilgrimage to the Holy Lands

Tariq has also performed Hajj and Umrah along with his family. When he reached the city of Mecca, the feeling was beyond words as he had a dream of coming here for years. He approached that goal in the best way that he knew how. He read books about Hajj; He went to classes about Hajj; his wife and he planned out every step of our itinerary including where they would be after Hajj was over just to make sure we covered all of our bases. And needless to say, much of his focus was on the mechanics of it all – the proper way in which to make Tawaaf, the proper surahs to recite in the Rakahs, the proper haircuts to get done, and the appropriate places to be at the appropriate times, etc. All in all, he had read just about every Hajj Manual out there and was pretty sure he knew most of the *fiqh* rulings that would come into play while he was on this most sacred of journeys.

Taking part in the pilgrimage at least once in one's lifetime is a major obligation for all Muslims and Tariq was fortunate in term of financial and physical means. He also received the greatest opportunity to touch the Kabba. He also met with Imam of Khana-e- Kaaba Sheikh Abdullah Bin Subil and Masjid-e- Nabwi. They hand over the heads of children, especially Shazia.

It was at this moment Tariq felt a surge of something moving inside him, he was touching the symbol that he had spent all of his life praying towards. Before performing Hajj, he read the guidebook called Manasik-e-Hajj, which is a breakdown of the Hajj rituals and the spiritual meaning behind each act. "After his Hajj, he intended to try his utmost hardest to live the life of a better person, but before he does that he needed to ask for forgiveness and cleaned his heart. So he viewed his hajj as a spiritual refuel of energy, which should aid and assist him in living the rest of his life just the way he was supposed to.

On the 8th of Dhul-Hijjah, they all entered ihram, which is wearing plain clothes. After this, all of them headed towards Mina by foot and traveled 8km journey. The spent the whole day in mina and offered prayers and spend most of the time remembering Allah. After this came the most important day, The Day of Arafat. The Mount Mercy at Arafat was the scene of Prophet Muhammad's (Peace Be Upon Him) final sermon. After making 14.4 km journey to Mina, they spent the day at Arafat in reverent prayer. After sunset, it was time to move towards Muzdalifah which was a 9 km journey, where they spent the night under stars. Most of the people started collecting pebbles here and departed again just before the sunrise. Then came yum-ul Hajj, the longest day of the pilgrimage.

They celebrated Eid-ul-Adha on 10th of Dhul-Hajj. Their day started in Muzdalifah and then they headed back to Mina before dawn. In Mina they performed the first rami, throwing seven pebbles at the largest of three columns known as Jamarat. It is believed that at this spot in Mina, the devil appeared and tried to dissuade Abraham from heeding the command. Abraham responded by throwing stones to scare him off. After casting their stone, they performed the sacrifice.

Completing the story, when Abraham went to sacrifice his son, he found God had placed a ram there to be slaughtered instead. They slaughtered a goat and pay for it to be done in their name. At this point, men shaved their heads and removed their ihrams. After this they proceeded towards Mecca to perform Tawaf and Sa'ee, first circling the Kabba seven time and then walking seven-time between the hills of Safa and Marwa. When all was done they headed back to their campsite in Mina. When their time in Mina was finished, they returned to Mecca to perform the final circulation of the Kaaba, a "farewell" tawaf.

"Hajj ingrained in me the importance of being compassionate to others and to treat them fairly, to be humble before the Almighty, it acts as a constant reminder to persevere and have faith in Allah during times of need and despair as well as to be patient when faced with any test. Even though I went with my family, I came back forming new bonds with pilgrims who would later be like family and we continue visiting one another regularly," says Tariq.

Tariq with his wife and children Fouzia, Atif and Saquib at Masjid-e-Ayesha for Umrah

Tariq was blessed enough to perform Umrah in the month of Ramadan. The holy month that is full of blessings where a Muslim get spiritual and mental relief. Tariq talked about his experience, "the sweet taste of carrying out Umrah in the month of Ramadan was further motivated during five daily prayers. Especially during Taraweeh when gorgeous Mosque Al-Haram was sparkling and bright with masses equal to those present at Hajj. This whole experience became more spiritual when you know that every one of the people is endeavoring and striving for the same journey, i.e., to seek the blessing of Allah Almighty and forgiveness. Every passing day made my journey more spiritual and memorable, and for most of the pilgrims, it was the Ramadan of a lifetime. Ramadan has always been a sharing event. Millions around the world take shelter with Allah from the evil and the bad selves. Muslims all over the world plead to Allah and ask for mercy. For the whole month, Muslims fast and say prayers. The objective of all the prayers and the fasting is for Allah. Every person wants to ensure that they spend their time reading the Quran and being good to their kin and family. The bounties of Allah (SWT) are already increased manifold during the holy month of Ramadan such that each virtue is rewarded 70 to 700 times more than its normal reward. When these two acts come together, one can fathom how lucky and blessed the individual is who gets a chance to perform Umrah in Ramadan. The first thing that came to my mind was a kindness. I was able to breakfast with different people from all across the world each day. It was amazing. I was never able to know that so many people have the same meaning towards life. And that was an eye-opener. I remember a man from Sudan insisting to open fast with me, I was humbled. Tears and tears. I was scared and delighted at the same time. No other place in the world would allow me to be happy and sad at the same time. I was happy because I was finally in the house of Allah, says Tariq.

Tariq with his wife Parveen, daughter Fouzia, sons Shariq and Atif, mother in law and nephew Khalid and Khalid's best friend Lateef at Muzdalifah- Makkah, Saudi Arabia

Conveying his feeling for this opportunity Tariq expressed, "Due to the importance of Ramadan, people want to anticipate in the beautiful procession of Umrah. It is just adding or even multiplying your good deeds. What a beautiful way to spend Ramadan. Imagine the opportunity to be close to the holiest shrines and places during the holy month. It is a rare opportunity and must be availed by people across the world. "There is a lot more one learns from Hajj which nobody can explain. Tariq learned how to give and not react if something goes against my will. It taught him how to endure pain and still keep a smiling face. It taught him how to respect the others who go through difficult times. It taught him that in the eyes of Allah, those who have paid money for a VIP hajj are similar to the ones sleeping on the mountains without any cover.

Role Model

Tariq has learned a lot from the life of Prophet Muhammad (Peace Be Upon Him). Prophet Muhammad (Peace Be Upon Him) is the role model for Tariq and indeed he's the best role model for all mankind because he had a good moral character. Also, the Prophet Muhammad (Peace Be Upon Him) was the best teacher, the best friends, the best father, the best husband and the best guardian of the orphans. Tariq has learned from the life of Prophet Muhammad (Peace Be Upon Him) and the countless examples which show his status as a role model for all the Muslims, societies and individuals. His life was dominated by a superior morality, good habits, noble and gentle feelings, all of which are the characteristics that help prevent people from getting entangled in sins. He has learned the lesson of leadership as the Holy Prophet of Islam possessed the status of divine leadership and his manners in dealing with people. "He had no love for luxuries or the illusion of this mortal world. He was never enchanted by any worldly things, and he invariably looked upon his world's life as a passing one, Tariq explained.

If there is any person that has lived on the face of this earth who was complete in every regard and the life of whom can serve as a beacon of guidance people in every walk of life, that personality undeniably is Prophet Muhammad (Peace Be Upon Him). Prophet Muhammad (Peace Be Upon Him) was a selfless as a person could be in his life. All of his undertakings and motives were just to fulfill the order of

Allah. He was the epitome of good manners and his every action in life was the representation of highest morals and manners that a person could exhibit. He is an Ideal being in terms of manners and ethics, the likes of which the world has not seen, says Tariq.

He also learned the lessons of tolerance and forgiveness as Prophet Muhammad (Peace Be Upon Him) never attempted to retaliate against the insults and disrespect of anyone, and forgave people's mistakes and their misconduct. His reaction towards the torment and disregard of the ignorant people was always forgiveness and tolerance. "He was responsible for both the theology of Islam and its main ethical and moral principles and in many other respects, in short, a model to be followed universally in all aspects of life for man. In addition, He played the key role in establishing the religious practices of Islam, "says Tariq.

Speaking about his role model Tariq said, "The personality of Prophet Muhammad (Peace Be Upon Him) has touched my heart like no other personality. I have had a life-longed association with his life, words, actions, and behavior; however, not a day in my life passes without my love for the Prophet (Peace Be Upon Him) increasing. The Prophet (Peace Be Upon Him) is my source of inspiration for my connection with Allah. I find myself closer to Allah as I awake to his words. As I accomplish my tasks and derive satisfaction from my achievements, I am reminded never to allow myself to slip into a feeling of vainglory - the Prophet's (Peace Be Upon Him) complete humility during his greatest moment of victory, as Makkah fell into his hands, can never be forgotten. I marvel at the charisma he possessed whereby hundreds of men and women would only refer to him as their beloved, and gave the impression that no matter how eloquent they were, their words could not fully describe his magnanimity, nobility of character, and benevolence. I find no leader who won his enemies over to his cause through the nobility of character and magnanimity as he did. Their number and affiliations varied: chiefs of tribes, kings, commanders, orators, men, and women of all backgrounds and ages. Their enmity transformed into passionate love for him and his cause - as if through a miracle."

Favorite Sports Personality

Talking about his most admired sports personality Tariq mentioned the Jahangir Khan, the world's no 1 squash player from Pakistan. Jahangir Khan was born on 10th December in Karachi was originally from Peshawar. During his career, he won the World Open six times and British Open ten times. From 1981, 1986, he was unbeaten in competitive plays. During that time he won 555 matched consecutively, the longest winning streak played by any athlete in top-level professional sports as recorded in Guinness World Records. "I grew up reading reports of Jahangir Khan and even then he seemed a mythical, magical figure to me," said Tariq. Jahangir Khan was the man whose name was an alternative word with Squash. A man is commonly known as the world's best performer ever and a sportsperson who excelled in his sports to be recognized as the world's greatest ever sportsman. A man who set the bar so high that very few others have come close. Tariq was inspired by how Jahangir Khan continued playing even when the doctors advised him not to take part in any physical activity. He was very weak as a child underwent Hernia operation, but his family let him play their family game. In 1979, when the selectors decided not to select Jahangir to take part in Worlds Championships in Australia, refereeing him too weak from current illness. He then decided to go to the World Amateur Individual Championship and at the age of 15, he became the youngest ever winner of that event.

A rare photo of Tariq while meeting Jahangir Khan

Jahangir Khan took the world by awe in the squash arena and his achievement inspired. Despite facing a lot of hardships in his sports career, it was his passion for sports that Jahangir get along with hard work and dedication which made it all possible for him to overcome the obstacles. Jahangir who was considered by many to be a great player in the history of the game was also the fittest player in the game. It was his vigorous training regime consisted of running, playing squash and exercising in the gym that made him invincible. He would cover 10 miles a day in short and long-distance running, and would train for seven to eight hours each day", says Tariq.

Jahangir Khan was told that he would never become the world champion. He was the youngest, smallest, feeblest and the sickest of all the family. No one believed that there was a chance for Jahangir to become a good squash player. Having gone from such unpromising beginnings to become one of the greatest players of all time- he is now an inspiration for everyone. Through bravery, willpower and individual sacrifice, Jahangir overcame personal tragedy and eventually excel at the world's most physically challenging sport. All of this did not come easily. Jahangir's father was informed by the doctors that he would not be able to play any sport because of his surgeries. He had even come to a point in his career when he decided to quit the sport. This was when his elder brother and mentor Torsam khan who was also a world champion before he died from heart attack. Jahangir was extremely close to his brother and his death affected him and he decided to quit the game, but later changed his decision only to live out his brother's dream.

Mr. Tariq and Qamar Zaman (World Squash Champion) invited as guests in Squash Tournament

Muhammad Tariq Khan is among the most famous badminton personalities. He was invited as a guest in a Squash Tournament held in Karachi. Mr. Qamar Zaman who is the world Squash Champion was also invited in the tournament. Squash enthusiasts came together for a day of fun and camaraderie while enjoying a sport they love. New players got the chance to experience the feel of playing competitively while advanced players showcased their skills and won fantastic prizes, says Tariq.

Favorite Political Personality

From the political perspective, Tariq most favorite personality was Quaid-e-Azam Muhammad Ali Jinnah. Tariq admired Quaid-e-Azam because he was the most revered leader of the Muslims of the Subcontinent. A man having a strong moral unmatched by any modern leader of those times. According to Tariq, some people are born great, some achieve greatness and others have greatness thrust upon them, but Jinnah qualifies all the criteria of being a great leader. Quaid was a lawyer, politician and a great visionary whose immense struggle made the tough task of the foundation of a Muslim state possible on 14th August 1947. Tariq says that Quaid-e-Azam had the confidence to stand alone, the courage to make tough decisions and the compassion to listen to the needs of others. He was a great and visionary leader who not the only paved way to establish the concept of nationhood for Muslims of Subcontinent but his farsightedness for having a separate home proved true. He had the power to win the hearts through open, speech and vote and that's how he achieved the dream of one nation.

Tariq expressed that we are indeed a blessed nation to have Quaid-e-Azam as our leader. Tariq says that if Muslims look back and think what kind of power Jinnah gave us in the form of independent country, we cannot thank enough for such blessings as nations which are striving for their identity are suffering badly in dominating hands and those who have the freedom must acknowledge this great gift. Tariq respected Quaid-e-Azam because he was the man of principles. He never compromised on his beliefs and principles. Talking about his personality Tariq said, "He was the most remarkable man of his time. Throughout his whole life, not even his enemies were able to point a finger at him. It was because of his wise leadership that Muslim of the subcontinent got Pakistan with the ballot and not with a bullet. He always fought with the British and Hindus politically with great courage and bravery. It was his courage and bold leadership which made him a great leader.

Quaid-e-Azam always advocated freedom for women and encouraged them to come forward and take part in social work when they were able to find the time, without neglecting their domestic obligations and tasks for their children. His sister, Fatima Jinnah, accompanied him to most of his public meeting and was also seated near to home on the dais. God had granted him a quality which I had not seen in any Indian Muslim: He is incorruptible and un-purchasable.

Closure

Tariq has led a very successful and fulfilling life. The day he moved to Pakistan ... that area was attacked, and many were killed and injured but his family had left about two hours before. Partition marked a massive and bloody upheaval. Millions of Muslims abandoned their homes to cross the border into Pakistan. All those years hold tremendous importance in Tariq's life. With determination and hard work, Tariq achieved his goals and desire to become a Badminton Champion. His idea of success is just living a humble, happy life surrounded by those who love you and have the freedom to do what you love. His life might be a simple life now, but it is a happy one, and it is a fulfilling one. There is nothing that can stop us from achieving what we want in life. Our only obstacle is ourselves and the extent of our ability to differentiate between a worthwhile goal and self-destructive goal.

About the Author

S usan Hill is an English author and short-story writer whose production initially stretched its top in late 1960's and early 1970's. Her merely strained novels observe the lives of small, at times eccentric individuals who look for life and warmth in their often frozen and sterile lives. She was born in 1942 to R.H and Doris Hill in Scarborough, a working-class city on the east shore of England. Hill joined the grammar school in Scarborough and Coventry and graduated with honors in English from King's College, the University of London in 1963. After her graduation, she reviewed books for the Coventry Evening Telegraphy till 1969, when she became a permanent critic, writer, and broadcaster. In 1975, Hill married the Shakespeare scholar Stanley Wells. They had a daughter and lived in Royal Leamington Spa, Oxfordshire and Warwickshire. Hill's most of the stories are inscribed in a dramatic gothic style, particularly her ghost story *The Woman in Black*, published in 1983. She has also exhibited interest in traditional English flicker stories that relies on suspense and atmosphere to make its influence to the typical ghost stories. In 1987, this novel was turned into a play to continue to run in West End of London. The novel was also made a television film in 1989 and a film by Hammer Film Productions in 2012. In 2004, Hill created a sequence of crime stories featuring investigator Simon Serrailler, titled *The Various Haunts of Men* (2004). Hill was bestowed with Somerset Maugham Award (1971), the Whitbread Literary Award

(1972) and the Rhys Memorial Prize (1972). Hill has lately started her own publishing firm, Long Barn Books that has published two Simon Serrailler short stories and The Magic Apple Tree, as well as The Dream Coat and Coloring In.